D1818415

PORIBORTON!

Ruchir Joshi is a film-maker and writer based in Kolkata. He is the author of *The Last Jet-Engine Laugh* and the editor of *Electric Feather*, a compilation of contemporary Indian erotica.

Poriborton!

An Election Diary

RUCHIR JOSHI

HarperCollins *Publishers* India
a joint venture with

THE INDIA TODAY GROUP

New Delhi

For Mihirda,
Hoping you'll enjoy
this.
With my regards,
Ruchir.
Calcutta, Jan '12

First published in India in 2011 by
HarperCollins *Publishers* India
a joint venture with
The India Today Group

Copyright © Ruchir Joshi 2011

ISBN: 978-93-5029-167-2

2 4 6 8 10 9 7 5 3 1

Ruchir Joshi asserts the moral right
to be identified as the author of this work.

The views and opinions expressed in this book are the author's own and the facts
are as reported by him, and the publishers are not in any way liable for the same.

All rights reserved. No part of this publication may be reproduced,
stored in a retrieval system, or transmitted, in any form or by any means,
electronic, mechanical, photocopying, recording or otherwise,
without the prior permission of the publishers.

HarperCollins *Publishers*
A-53, Sector 57, NOIDA 201301, India
77-85 Fulham Palace Road, London W6 8JB, United Kingdom
Hazelton Lanes, 55 Avenue Road, Suite 2900, Toronto, Ontario M5R 3L2
and 1995 Markham Road, Scarborough, Ontario M1B 5M8, Canada
25 Ryde Road, Pymble, Sydney, NSW 2073, Australia
31 View Road, Glenfield, Auckland 10, New Zealand
10 East 53rd Street, New York NY 10022, USA

Typeset in ITC Stone Serif Std 10.5/14
InoSoft Systems Noida

Printed and bound at
Thomson Press (India) Ltd.

CONTENTS

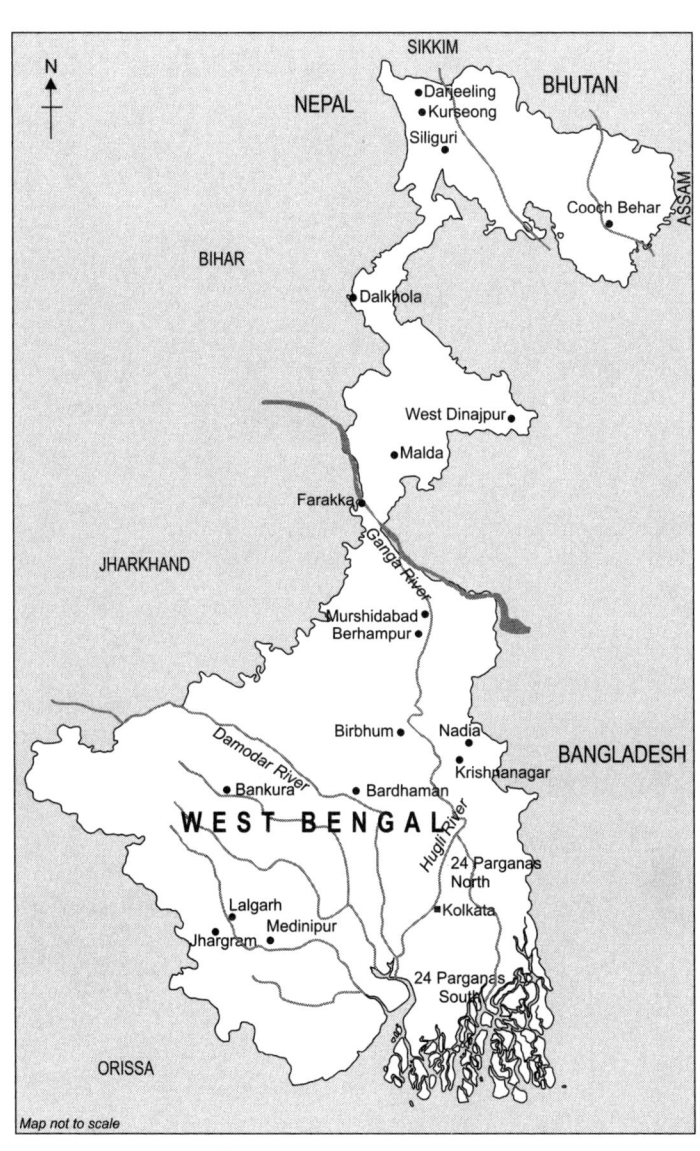

N

SIKKIM

NEPAL

BHUTAN

• Darjeeling
• Kurseong
Siliguri

Cooch Behar

ASSAM

BIHAR

• Dalkhola

West Dinajpur •

• Malda

Farakka •

Ganga River

JHARKHAND

Murshidabad •
Berhampur •

Birbhum •

Nadia •

Krishnanagar •

BANGLADESH

Damodar River

• Bankura

• Bardhaman

W E S T   B E N G A L

Hugli River

24 Parganas
North

Lalgarh •

Medinipur •

• Kolkata

Jhargram •

24 Parganas
South

ORISSA

Map not to scale

Dramatis Personae

Mamata Banerjee: 'firebrand leader', 'loose cannon'; 'saviour of Bengal', at the end of the elections described in this book; now, finally, chief minister of West Bengal. From the working-class end of the middleclass, Banerjee started her political career as Youth Congress worker; rose to defeat the communist stalwart Somnath Chatterjee in parliamentary elections; split with the Congress to form her own party, the Trinamool Congress or TMC; aligned herself with the BJP for a while, before realigning with the Congress; and this May, defeating the Left Front in Bengal. AKA: Didi, MamBan, Netri, MB, etc.

Buddhadeb Bhattacharya: the CPM leader who took over from Jyoti Basu and ruled West Bengal for over a decade, till Mamata Banerjee defeated him. AKA: BB, Com B, etc.

Pranab Mukherjee: old Congress high command who has held many different portfolios; known as a steady hand and troubleshooter from the time of Indira Gandhi.

Adhir Chowdhury: Congress leader and MP from Murshidabad who refused to play nice with the Trinamool in the seat distribution for state elections in his area despite instructions from Delhi. Chowdhury fielded four 'independent' candidates against the CPM and the TMC. The idea was that the Congress would accept them back the moment they won. All four lost to the TMC.

Biman Bose: secretary of the state CPM and chairman of the Left Front, apparently the most doctrinaire of the CPM leadership.

Subhash Ghising: aging leader of the Gorkha National Liberation Front (GNLF) whose 1980s campaign for Gorkhaland set fire to the hill areas and shook the Left Front government in Kolkata.

Bharati Tamang: widow of the Gorkha leader Madan Tamang who was stabbed to death in front of the Planters' Club in Darjeeling in 2010.

Roshan Giri: general secretary of the leading Gorkha party, the Gorkha Janamukti Morcha (GJM).

Dawa Lama: treasurer of the GJM.

Trilok Dewan: former chief secretary of Andhra Pradesh, now a victorious MLA for the GJM.

Derek O'Brien: leader of the TMC and member of Mamata Banerjee's closest circle of advisors.

Prosenjit Bose: head of the CPM's Research Cell in New Delhi; a rare young person among the aging party leadership.

Anil Basu: CPM leader and former MP from Arambagh constituency who lost his seat when the TMC mauled the CPM in the 2009 parliamentary elections.

Gautam Deb: CPM leader and, it was heavily rumoured, the man who was supposed to replace Buddhadeb Bhattacharya as chief minister a few months after the elections. Deb garnered the most coverage of any CPM leader during the elections and it was he who first made the accusation that the TMC was receiving black and foreign money.

Fatima: a social worker in Howrah.

B: journalist for a vernacular newspaper.

Manoj Mahato: a young leader of the People's Committee against Police Atrocity (PCPA) in Lalgarh, Medinipur. The PCPA is a party accused by opponents of being close to Maoists.

Shyamal: a member of the PCPA.

Bimal Pandey: brother of Anuj Pandey, who is accused of leading one of the murderous Harmad gangs associated with the CPM. Anuj Pandey is absconding after the police issued a warrant against him.

Dukkhoshyam Chitrakar, **Gurupada Chitrakar** and **Suvarna Chitrakar**: singer-painters who make the traditional Bengali narrative scrolls.

PS: a political scientist.

PT: a political theorist.

Planned Escapes

By mid-February, the prognosis looks very bad. The weather in Kolkata is alien, still cool, with no trace of the heat that usually sends its first visiting cards by the end of January. While many foolish people would look at this as a good thing, Kolkata veterans know that all an extended 'spring' signifies is a particularly brutal summer. The World Cup is about to begin, but, again, every sensible person knows that this Indian team has little chance of getting past the quarter-finals. Looking ahead, it's clear what's going to happen in March: the hot weather is going to kick in just as India go down – yet again – to ignominious defeat; the kids are going to suffer through their Board exams; the state elections are going to be declared and the tinder-keg called 'rural Bengal' or 'outside Kolkata' is going to explode into scattered but regular violence. By April, things are going to be hellish. I've already spoken to friends who have a house in Himachal Pradesh and am looking at the availability of train and plane tickets. I'm hoping to get away to my friends' TV-free house before I'm forced to watch the WC final on 2 April between two teams that are not India. I'm also hoping to completely avoid the mess of the election campaign as things get ugly between the ruling Left Front and the challengers, Trinamool Congress.

The call from *The Telegraph* is innocuous enough. I write a regular freelance column for their edit page but, this once, they want me to attend the annual *Telegraph* Debate where Mamata Banerjee will be speaking and write about it for their front page the next day. I've never seen Mamata 'live' and I'm curious to see how she handles herself in this company. The rest of the line-up of usual suspects looks like they could also provide some entertainment. The clincher is the dinner afterwards where I'll get to meet Rahul Dravid, who's one of the debaters. So, I agree.

18

The Telegraph Debate

On the evening of 18 February, the lights are bright around the entrance to the Netaji Subhash Indoor Stadium. Cops are checking passes, college students are trooping in, school students too, complete with little notebooks, TV crews are filming. Just behind the Indoor Stadium sulks big brother Eden Gardens, dark concrete ramparts looming, shamefully declared unready to take on the one big match assigned to it in the forthcoming World Cup. Inside the arena, people are settling down in a buzz of expectancy. Near the stage, a TV crew is making practice sweeps with its crane-jib. I get the news that Victor Bannerjee, actor and orator, is not going to make it to the debate; he has been replaced by Suhel Seth, Kolkata's biggest gift to the schmooze-networks of New Delhi. As the camera swoops down again, it narrowly misses the head of Derek O'Brien, Emperor of Quizland and one of Mamata's core team, as he and another man sidle into the seats next to me.

'Hi Ruchir!'

'Hi Derek, do you know Victor Bannerjee's been replaced by Suhel Seth?'

Derek smiles. 'Suhel is capable of replacing any of the speakers on either side, except My Leader!'

'Arre, why yaar?' I counter cheerfully, 'put him in a sari and I'm sure he'll replace her also!'

Derek and his wingman snap their heads away from me as if they've been stung by wasps. Even though my intention was to underline the chameleon nature of Seth and his PR skills, it's clearly not done to joke about Their Leader.

As the speakers take their seats on either side of the stage, I realize that there's no one at all from the Left Front, on stage or off. Clearly, neither the CPM nor anyone else from the Baam Front has been invited to attend this particular party. Or maybe they were invited and declined.

'In the opinion of the house, India will be better run if politicians are left out of the government.' It's the kind of motion that could swing either way. It could easily degenerate into a deadly dull exchange of banalities or it could be a platform for some pretty interesting stuff.

Luckily for all of us, it's the latter. Aveek Sarkar, the owner of *Ananda Bazar Patrika* and managing editor of

The Telegraph, begins with introductory remarks about each of the debaters that suggest irreverence is being invited rather than avoided and, intentionally or not, most of the speakers do not disappoint.

Speakers for the motion, i.e., against politicians running anything are: Suhel Seth (PR Man who hobnobs with politicians, especially Arun Jaitley of the BJP), Rahul Dravid (cricketer), Dipankar Gupta (sociologist) and Swapan Dasgupta (de facto Angrezi-speaking spokesperson and general frontman for the BJP). Speaking against the motion, i.e., backing the idea that things should be run by politicians, are Ramachandra Guha (historian), Jay Panda (politician), Salman Khursheed (politician) and Mamata Banerjee (Mother of all Politicians).

Suhel Seth is first to the podium. Avoiding any mention of his own friends in politics, Seth launches into the badness of politicians in general and Congress politicians in particular – QED the country should get rid of all politicians who are not in the Sangh Parivar. He looks at Mamata Banerjee and informs her that she is a great leader but that she probably won't make a great chief minister. You can tell from his tone and the way he glances at Mamata that he's likely warned someone in the Trinamool that he will say something like this in order to appear critical and that they shouldn't mind. Next, Seth rails against corrupt 'dark-glass-wearing leaders of southern states' (clearly, his pals, north Indian politicians who wear shades, are all right) and, finally, takes a hard swipe at the PM, Manmohan Singh, thundering: 'He doesn't know between which stools he stands!' From Seth's strained voice, one can gauge that his own relationship with stools is a bit iffy too. Summary: Politicians are bad; bad politicians are really bad; politics itself isn't all bad.

Ram Guha walks up first for the side defending the right of politicians to exist. Despite his deficit of ancient years, Guha has now perfected what one can only term a faux-geriatric, Hobsbawmesque demeanour. If it weren't for politicians, says Guha, no one on the opposite panel save Rahul Dravid would have a job. We have to thank the politicians who made our Constitution and so does Rahul Dravid, for, otherwise, he would have ended up playing for a country called 'Mysore State'. Guha then rapidly swings at all the non-politicians we've allowed into power, ranging from the really bad ones (Sanjay Gandhi, failed entrepreneur) to good people (good old PM, fine economist but clueless politician) and then settles on Mamata Banerjee as a proper kind of politician, one who's risen from the people by fighting and winning elections.

By the end of the evening, Ram Guha is proved absolutely right and Suhel Seth demonstrably destroyed.

Once Mamata Banerjee stands up to speak, the real lines of the debate become very clear: on one side is this selection of English-speaking men, with their posh voices ranging from Seth and Dasgupta's high whines to Guha, Gupta and Khursheed's baritones, on the other side there is Mamata, stepping down the pitch and smacking everyone to all parts of the ground.

Swapan Dasgupta has earlier gone on his usual attack against his favourite bugbear, 'Nehruvian hangovers', fumbling badly with the word 'kalyug' like a butter-fingered slip fielder with a hot edge. (Once, Punjabi style 'kll-yoog', then the Brown Saheb in him coming out with 'call-yugg' and then, in his excitement, the final murder of Hindi, the word becoming simply 'cull-yooo'.) MamBan grabs him first by the scruff of the neck: 'I will see the Swapan Dasgupta's face on TV all the time protecting the BJP!' and 'There are some bad people, there are some goody-goody people who don't take risks ... they are not politicians but *shadow* politicians!' Then she turns to Dravid who has suggested that politicians should be 'dropped' not just for corruption but also bad performance. 'Bhai? Don't you have in cricket both batting and also betting?' and then, one of the killer lines of the evening: 'Tell me bhai! Without ball can you play cricket? Rossogolla with salt? Newspaper without headline? Country without leader?'

Her voice goes into the standard Bengali Politician's Rising Shriek as she names some past greats of Indian and Bengal politics, Bhagat Singh, Gandhi, Subhash, etc. 'Can you *ignore*?' she shouts, meaning can you ignore these names? '... Pollution-free politics! May not be Hurvaard, may not be knowing batting or bowling but, bhai, they know good fielding!'

To all the anti-politicians (except, presumably, Swapan Dasgupta), MB then summarily offers: 'Come to my party! Stand for election! Suhel-ji, come! I will give you a ticket! I will give you all tickets!' In short, put your money where your mouth is, come put yourself on the line. If not, shut up. Then in the crescendo comes this ace of aces for the people who refuse to commit themselves openly: 'These Shadow Politicians!' She waves across the stage. 'They are trying to control the government from the *backside*!'

Ultimately, for all of Salman Khursheed's buttered debatery, for all of Swapan Dasgupta's semi-skimmed demagoguery, for all of Guha's warmly intimate quotations and anecdotes, and for all of Dipankar Gupta's smooth reasoning, this other Kolkata has one answer: 'Because you are having a good command in your English language ...' hard shake of head, '... but you have to think of the poor people also!' Huge applause from the audience that I'm sure consists of a majority who also have a reasonable command over their English. So much then for Burke and Churchill, St Stephen's College, Cambridge and Oxford, who collectively take a hard kick on the backside.

It is brilliant, it is scary, and it may yet prove to be the harbinger of darker and funnier things.

Later that evening, I arrive late at the promised dinner, having had to make a detour to file my story. When I get there, the table has already been laid with one of the most sumptuous buffets you are likely to get in Kolkata, a mix of upper-five-star catering and the house's own legendary *Bangla ranna*. The wine is still flowing and the suit-boots are milling around in small groups, the participants of the debate still looking somewhat shell-shocked.

I chat with a couple of the suits I know before managing to get myself introduced to Rahul Dravid. An affable man, Dravid seems only too happy to discuss the prospects of this World Cup in which he's not playing. We talk about the huge chunk of time the tournament will take out of all our lives and Dravid is very clear about his strategy. 'No way am I going to watch all the league matches. I've got kids, you know. I guess I'll start watching seriously from the knock-out stage.' 'But that's another whole fortnight!' I'm about to point out when I locate MamBan on my peripheral vision. She's sitting in one corner of the wood-panelled dining room. She seems to be eating nothing. Every now and then somebody is invited to approach her and she chats with him for a while. The person leaves and another one is granted audience; there is clearly no question of mingling with the people she has just publicly mangled. After a while, looking carefully, I notice Madam *is* eating something – every now and then she takes handfuls of dry muri, puffed rice, from a bowl, and flicks it into her mouth, her eyes never leaving the gathering.

Later, someone tells me Mamata is a devotee of Santoshi Ma and therefore doesn't eat proper food on Fridays. Still later, I ask someone what would have happened if MamBan had spoken earlier in the debate and one or two of the opposing team had had a chance to rebut her. 'No chance. Her first condition for agreeing to take part in the debate was that she got to speak last.' I remember Mamata's balefully observant stare when I hear this. The lady may fast and pray for the blessings of whichever deity but she wasn't about to depend on anything other than good, hard-nosed, earthly political sense to make sure no Good-English-command-suit-boot got in the last word on her.

March arrives and progresses with mixed-up deliveries of the expected and the unexpected. Against all history, the weather remains strangely cool. The elections are duly declared by the election commissioner on the thirteenth of the month, as the latest five-year term of the Left Front government starts to reach its end. The Trinamool, led by Mamata Banerjee, welcomes the announcement and begins the predictable pre-election cat and mouse with the opponents and the media: 'There will be an alliance with the Congress,' 'Oh no, there won't, we don't need them,' 'Of course, we will look at Sonia-ji and Manmohan-ji as our allies, but only if the terms are correct,' and so on. The one surprise is that MamBan herself refuses to take up a seat to fight: 'I'm needed by my party to campaign all over the state; if the people elect us, I will take oath as chief minister and stand in a by-election a few months later.' Unspoken but clear in huge neon is the opposite: 'And if we fail to come to power, I will stay on as railway minister in the Centre.'

The other oddball in the mix is that the elections in West Bengal are to be held across nearly a month, from 17 April to result day on 13 May, with different groups of districts assigned polling days in six different phases to allow the paramilitary forces to move down from one end of the state to the other. This method has been put into practice in other states, and a truncated version of it was deployed in the 2009 Lok Sabha polls here, but this is the first time the method is being employed in West Bengal state elections. Yet another oddball is that no loudspeakers are to be allowed till after the school kids' Board exams which end in mid-April; this snatches away the main electioneering instrument used by all the parties – the amplifier and loudspeaker, either on stage or mobile on trucks, vans and cycle-rikshas – till three days before the Phase-1 vote in north Bengal. Even as we digest all this, the main thing that's destabilizing the kids' Board exams springs the biggest surprise of the month: India first whip Australia in the WC quarter-finals without breaking a sweat, then they beat Pakistan in the semis without changing gear, with almost as much ease, putting them in the finals against Sri Lanka at Wankhede Stadium, Mumbai, on 2 April. Of course, we still aren't going to win the Cup but this run itself has been bonus-miraculous, and when we lose, at least it won't be to England, Australia, South Africa or, horror of horrors, Pakistan.

Just as no candidate can get to the US presidency while admitting to atheism, or, indeed, to any other religion but Christianity, no major politician in India can actually say, 'I hate cricket. I don't understand it. It bores the fuck out of me.'

Across the business end of the World Cup, it becomes clear that Didi doesn't do cricket. Through the quarters and semis and up to the final, she maintains a sphinx-like silence, except to say, 'I support the Indian team and I wish them the best of luck.' What I start liking about MamBan during this time is that she doesn't suddenly develop a love for the game or pretend to watch the matches on TV. As the nation and the city do their mass nail-biting, Mamata Banerjee, Uber-Didi, supposed chief-minister-in-waiting occupies herself by ... painting. On the day India play Australia, she completes, according to some reports, seven big canvases. Against Pakistan the fever mounts and she apparently finishes ten paintings on the day. The day after the final against Sri Lanka, nobody bothers to send in a count.

I watch the Sri Lanka game with friends in Bhawanipur. As Dhoni dhoka-fies the winning runs, the nation and all its far-flung India-islands erupt with joy. More than any other emotion, I find myself feeling intense relief that Sachin Tendulkar will not finish his career without holding the World Cup. Walking back the

short distance to my flat, I see that upper-middle-class Kolkata thinks differently – this is clearly the high point in the lives of hundreds of youth packing Elgin Road in their cars, clearly their 1983, after which everything will no doubt seem dull, downhill and unrewarding. Shouts of 'India! Indiaa! Indiaaaa!' rip through the balmy night air, the voices fighting with the massed horns and gunning engines as the celebrating vehicles nudge into each other. On the pavements, befuddled labourers sit up and rub their eyes as the sudden street-party wakes them up from their sleep, just as it did twenty-eight years ago when India won the Cup at Lord's. On the crossing of Elgin and Sarat Bose Road, kids are jumping on the bonnets of cars, teenage girls are pogo-ing out of sun-roofs; various avatars of the tricolour are being put through their paces, the pieces of cloth mobile, somehow streaking through jammed traffic. For a moment it feels like one imagines Buenos Aires or Rio must feel after Argentina or Brazil win the football World Cup, except there's no booze to be seen and the people are wearing far too many clothes.

The average age of those out on the streets is about twenty-two. Most of this crowd have never before lived through a time when India were – all too briefly – World Champions, and they've never lived in a West Bengal not ruled by the communists. As I reach home I find myself thinking that the minor tournament is now over, having ended the drought of twenty-seven years, and that the real gladiator battle opens tomorrow, to continue or finish something that's lasted thirty-four years. Will these same people also be celebrating come 13 May and the election results? Will the labourers who've been woken up by this brouhaha also then join them?

3

A Padayatra in Jadavpur

On this Sunday evening, just to the west of the Dhakuria bridge, there are at least five different species of police and security crowding the *gali* in front of an unprepossessing three-storey apartment building, probably built in the 1980s. It's an unlikely lair for an ageing but still deadly lion, but this is what Pranab Mukherjee, Hon'ble Finance Minister, Grandmaster of Photographic Memory, Senior Commander of the Congress, Legendary Baron of the Backroom, calls home.

Mingling among the police and security are about thirty members of the Fifth Estate, the cameras and microphones completely outgunning the Uniforms' weaponry. A black Santro is parked in front of the building, and near it stands a gaggle of healthy-looking middle-aged men, most of them in long kurtas, all of them exuding a kind of paunchy self-importance.

As I get there, a grizzled hack flips open his phone and conspires into it: *'Pranab-Mamata'r baithak shesh. Mamata kichhu boltey o paarey.'* A very public backroom powwow is just finishing in Pranab-babu's flat – between him and Mamata Banerjee – and the Wow is about to emerge and tell us what the Pow said.

When Mamata Banerjee comes out, she is engulfed by an instant tent made entirely of cameras and cameramen, a buzzing, jostling bee cluster around a particularly rewarding flower bush. Standing only four feet outside the *jhund*, it's impossible to hear what she's saying.

A denizen of south Kolkata, a man in his sixties, drives up from the other side of the gali in his newish-looking car and begins to hit his horn. A couple of khakis go over to inform the uncle about his position in life but the bhadralok refuses to accept it. *'Rasta-ta keno block korchhey?'* Why are they blocking the road?

Suddenly, the long-kurta Trinamool men explode into default rage. They rush shouting to the car and start bashing down on the roof and bonnet. One of them reaches inside to try and pull the insolent man out. The energy is scary: it's as if the man has tried to drive over Their Leader. Security snaps into overdrive. The Gyspies and Sumos fire up and jerk forward, right into the melee of press-wallas. A TV mike bounces on the ground, a Sumo tyre just missing it as MB is whisked away. The Trinamool men back off and the shaken old boy drives away slowly in his Hyundai. One of Pranab Babu's neighbours from the *basti* next door hikes up his lungi and asks no one in particular, 'What was that fool thinking? If this was a procession, tell me, could he have gone through? Chhaah!'

A bit later, standing on Dhakuria bridge, one can see a literal cross section of two different Kolkatas: squatting between the rail tracks below, a man chops into *daab*-shells, sorting them into piles, while children run across the sleepers from one shore of the old track-side slum to the other. On the bridge, the road is more or less quarantined of non-Mamata *janata*. Pedestrians are still using the sidewalk but the road itself has been cleared in both directions; clearly, no one except Trinamool's motorized infantry is allowed to drive on it. About ten Trinamool motorbikes are parked on the bridge, the men milling around, cheerful, sorting out the flags, waiting for their signal. A sweaty, exhausted-looking schoolboy walks past with his heavy cricket kit, his bat sticking out of the bag. After a few minutes, a cellphone rings, one of the men answers and then shouts to the rest of his comrades: Let's go. Didi is nearly on the bridge.

This is Mamata's fifth *padayatra* through the city and the idea is simple. No loudspeakers are allowed because of the Board exams, so she will walk with local candidates for a stretch of a few kilometres, but without saying anything. The padayatras have had mixed attendance, I'm told, with the one in north Kolkata being the most successful. Today's yatra seems to be topping that one. The abnormally cool evening air seems to warm up as the main procession from Gol

Park comes towards us and boils slowly up the bridge. First there are various clusters of Trinamool supporters shouting slogans; then the vans with tricolour balloons and styrofoam cut-outs of the ghastly child's drawing of the flower and two-leaf clover that is the party's symbol. *'Shaamne Kara? Trinomool! Pechhoney kara? TINommul!'* Who's ahead? Trinamool! Who's behind you? Trinamool! It's true, there's Trinamool in front and behind us. *'Daandikey kaara? Tinommool! Baanye kara? TEEnommoool!'* They *are* to our right, yes, but to the left, over the bridge parapet, the basti on the rail tracks continues its life, unmoved by the action above.

After waves of shouting, dancing party people comes Madam Didi herself. At first, one can't see her at all – from that tent of photographers outside Pranab Mukherjee's house she seems to have moved inside a mobile pandal of tri-coloured humans. Then, suddenly, I feel her before I see her. As she approaches, the procession spills over off the bridge road and on to the sidewalk, sweeping us up like an inefficient, start-stop, Kolkata-designed tsunami. Then, briefly, I can see the main cluster: Mamata is walking at the edge of a magical disc of asphalt that moves before her. It's actually the inner ring of volunteers keeping pace, forming an open circle around the Didi and the local candidates walking next to her. Just outside this ring is another ring, formed partly by Trinamool, partly by the security boys in the crisp safari suits, but largely by normal cops.

The Didi walks slowly, looking up, hands going into a *namaskar* every time she sees a building and balconies.

There are people in the high-rises around Dhakuria bridge and they wave to her and return the namaskar as she passes. At the end of the bridge there is a huge crowd waiting to receive her and we decide to take the narrow stairway off the bridge and overtake the core of the yatra.

Down the road past Jodhpur Park and Jadavpur, the chants create a web of sound. Except for the odd World Cup floppy and India shirt, it's as if the great victory at Wankhede happened a month ago and not last night; it's as if the real knock-out games have just begun today. Didi is not a great cricket fan and the only quarter given to the national vice is in a chant that I hear across the long procession: *'Dhakkkuria bolchhey, poriborton aashchhey, Jjjadavpur bolchhey, poriborton aashchhey!* Dhakuria says, change is on the way, Jadavpur says, change is on the way! And then, *'Shochin-Shewag bolchhey, poriborton aashchhey!'* And, taking note of Viru-beta's awful shot from last night and the new hero of the country, another man corrects the first sloganeer, *'Shochin-DHONI bolchhey, poriborton aashchhey!'*

As we walk along, a pattern gradually emerges. Clusters of people, some in ranks, some loose, then gaps and then more party faithful, elongating the whole procession, making it look bigger, taking possession of nearly seven kilometres of road all the way to Garia. At the side of the road are the bystanders, not necessarily won over yet, and sprinkled among them a heavy bandobast of khaki and black-white *mamas*, as Bengalis

affectionately call the local cops. At a point near the
8B bus stand there is a push from a kilometre away. A
man listens intently on his cellphone and then shouts,
'*Ei, taara taari egoe, Didi speed baadhiye diyechhey!*' Move
ahead, Didi has increased speed! Followed by a giggle
of triumph: we have a Didi who can surprise you, she
can speed up, unlike the opposition.

Passing the Sukanta Setu roundabout, I notice a single
red flag drooping, and then a solitary newly painted
hammer and sickle on a wall. Soon after begins the
static escort of shutdown factories, Sulekha, Krishna
Glass, Annapurna Glass, the built-over ghost of the old
Dabur estate. At Baghajatin, the dim lights give way.
There is a brightly lit, spanking new showroom in a
brand-new building. A row of shiny new Tata Nanos
stare down, ferret-like, watching the passing flood of
humans from their first-floor perch. '*Ek, Dui, Teen,
Chaar, CPM pankchaar!*' chants the crowd as it passes
the showroom. And then, still kicking at the great
departed icon of the Baamphont, '*Jyoti gelo paaliye,
teyish bochhor chaaliye, ebar jaabey Buddho, Bangla
hobey shuddho!*' Jyoti's run off, having managed it for
twenty-three years, now will go Buddha, Bengal will
be purified.

As the crowd accordions around me in the falling dusk,
I notice that the people are cheerful, pumped up, as
they say in sport, smelling victory already. There is
no sense at all of *duty bhorchhi,* none of the glazed,
bored looks that you see in some processions. As I try
and keep pace with the ebb and flow of the mass, I

wonder about the Trinamool gang in front of Pranab Mukherjee's house. Maybe some of those men were CPM when they were young. A couple of them were even old enough to have been among Priya Ranjan Das Munshi's Congress thugs during the Emergency in 1975.

5
APRIL

A Painting Exhibition on Theatre Road

A couple of days later, I find myself looking at an
exhibition of paintings at Gallerie 88 on Theatre Road.
The canvases in acrylic are mostly uniform, medium-
sized, with a few larger works interrupting the pattern
that spreads across the two small floors of the gallery.
At first glance, this is the worst kind of amateur
daubing, the kind of stuff done by the bored wife of a
corporate executive or a high-ranking army officer, just
enough knowledge to know what passes for 'modern'
art and nothing of the heart or skill needed to make
the images rise above the banal. But, as I look harder
at the paintings, I start to see something else. This
is actually childlike painting, there is no pretence at
presenting the paintings as anything other than what
they are. There are lots of flowers but some of the
flower pictures are monochrome, white on white, or
blue on blue, avoiding the deployment of every tube in

the paintbox, which is the mark of the truly hopeless wannabe artist. Occasionally, there is even a slash or splodge of pigment that's confident and, God help me, brings to mind various great painters. Howard Hodkin, David Hockney and even Philip Guston picked up from some turpentine ether.

As I walk through the exhibition I see red dots under most of the paintings. There are no images of suffering masses, this is what Mamata Banerjee does to get away from all that, this is clearly her semi-abstract, cricket-free utopia, her only known self-indulgence besides the occasional fried street snack. Idly, I try and calculate which and how many of these canvases MamBan painted as each succeeding game bringing India closer to the World Championship shut down her campaign.

On the first floor of the exhibition I see three people, two women and a man huddled around a table, sorting out postcard reproductions of the works. They look more like party workers than gallery assistants but I ask them how much the paintings are selling for. They look at me shiftily, as if I've accused them of something scandalous of which they are guilty. One of them points to a door. '*Bhetorey jigyesh korun.*' Please ask in there. I knock on the door and open it. There's a man inside, bothering some files. I ask him if I can have a price list. '*Shob* sold out,' he replies tersely, before turning back to his paperwork.

As I leave, I try and remember paintings made by the young Adolf Hitler and can't find any comparisons.

Next, I try the old Winston Churchill and his watercolour landscapes, but again, nothing matches. This is a mind and an eye of a different order and, try as I might, I can't really tell from these paintings whether the people of Bengal should be worried about a chief minister with a psycho condition or be relieved that their leader has recourse to a calming artistic hobby.

9
APRIL

Result Day (R-Day) minus 34

'But with a Bell as Well'
– Marginal People's Rally, Subodh Mullick Square

In 1972, the Congress defeated the second United Front government and recaptured Writers' Building. A bright young Bengali journalist buttonholed Kali Mukherjee, the legendary Congress dock-workers' leader, at the Press Club in Delhi. 'Kali-da, what will happen now that your party has come back to power?'

Kali-da recounted the story of a wandering sadhu who'd set up stall under the banyan tree outside a village. 'I can solve anybody's problems!' the babaji declared, 'just chant the mantra I give each of you individually!' Among the people who lined up was a recently married young woman who seemed unable to have children. The sadhu pondered over her problem and then asked her to come behind the banyan tree

to receive her secret mantra. Later, the girl's brother-in-law asked, 'Boudi, what mantra did the babaji give you?' The girl shrugged. 'Oh, exactly the same mantra your dada gives me every night, except the babaji rang a bell afterwards.'

Kali-da grinned at the journalist. *'Ebaar ki hobey? Jaa aagey hochhilo taai, shudhu ghonta baajiye!'* What will happen now? The same as before, except we'll ring a bell as well.

It's a story the few-thousand-odd people gathered at Subodh Mullick Square this Saturday afternoon seem to know all about. Here for the *Shramajibi Adhikaar Jatra*, they've come from all over the state: from the Sundarbans, from Medinipur, from the hill tracts up north, from the rolling graveyard of the dead tea-gardens in the Dooars, from Birbhum, Bardhaman and Bankura in the belly of Poschimbongo. Some have come from quite nearby as well: the hawkers from the city's streets and a union of sex workers from Sonagachhi. Looking around, it almost seems as though this is a part of a makeshift refugee camp put together after some natural calamity, except the variety of the people gathered indicates that this disaster cuts across many different geographies and, indeed, histories. This is the human tragedy distillation, not only of three decades of Left Front rule but also a few years of local Trinamool government. These are the West Bengal customers who are not buying the tickets or the cable connection to the ELL – the Election Lompho-Jhompo League or the Election Pantomime League.

Under a shamiana made from a patchwork of translucent white cement bags are clusters of colourful synthetic clothes. The cover overhead seems to trap heat rather than deflect it and the colours are drooping and still. Unlike the buoyant party rallies that have criss-crossed the city of late, the energy here seems low. Many of the people are lying down as they listen to the speeches, some of them deep in sweaty sleep, as if the heat has hammered them into the ground. At first glance you think this is exhaustion and despair, but if you look harder you see that these people are here for the long haul, a lifelong haul if need be, because they have no other choice.

As we look around the gathering, VR, the friend who's brought me here, remarks, 'You could also call this rally, "Where There's No Facebook".' VR, of course, is

taking off from David Werner's classic activist manual *Where There's No Doctor*, written while travelling in the most impoverished parts of South America, that tells people how to become their own doctors where no proper medical practitioners are available. Thinking about the wisecrack, I find myself in some awe at how so many people have managed to stay in touch using the simplest means of telephone, snail mail and representatives physically travelling from place to unconnected place.

As the various marching groups trickle in from the entry points around the city, Raj Kumar from Kurseong comes to the mike at the dais and speaks in Hindi. 'Saathiyon! Comrades!' His voice is high already and climbing, like a car starting in third gear. 'There are arrangements!' He points to his right, showing the way forward. 'The toilets! For women! Are on the right, over there!' He then declaims even more steeply. 'And! For the men! They are ... over there!' Then he says the same thing in Bangla and Nepali. My first reaction is to be amused that this man has no mode other than the comically melodramatic one favoured by most Bengali political leaders, even to make an announcement about toilets. Later, my amusement is replaced with a different understanding. Later, I realize something different.

As speaker after speaker comes up and introduces their group, an alternative map of Bengal starts to form under the hot shamiana, a barbed-wire grid of defunct factories and tea gardens, the workers abandoned, marginal fishermen displaced in Medinipur, city squatters evicted with no alternative housing offered, people suffering the pollutants from the sponge iron units in Durgapur, tribals and scheduled castes all under the cosh. This whole mass of people crushed by this 'People's government'. None of these issues making it into the Trinamool Congress manifesto or Didi's vision for a 'new Bengal'.

By the time Raj Kumar comes up to the mike again, I notice that there are no middle-class leaders in sight, no one with a *jhola* of urban sophistication and connections hanging off a simple kurta-pajama or handloom sari. 'As we stand at the gates of yet another election, the violence between these two parties grows while they both ignore our problems,' declaims Raj Kumar and I realize that this is his only mode of speech because he has no PR smoothness, no change of oratorial costume available to him – he is speaking to get across a message, not to sell himself as a speaker.

Walking through the crowd, I notice more and more people are sitting up now, some munching muri, some bananas, some drinking *lebu chaa*, tea with a squeeze of lime. As the azaan from the mosque next door ends, another speaker's voice becomes clear: '*Aamaader kono shelebrity nei*!' We have no celebrities. 'Those who work 365 days for us, they are our celebrities.' 'We don't want new laws, we just want you to implement the existing laws.' And, 'We want you to promise *only* what you can deliver!'

While they are asking for delivery, it's clear these groups have little hope in the mainstream parties. These people and their issues form the unyielding ground that electoral politics has never tried to turn. The easy promises that parties make bounce off the carapace of intractable problems. These are the *bonchito, shoshito, doridro, khetey-khaowa manush*, the very same 'deprived, excluded, exploited, labouring people' the CPM has always promised to liberate and empower and now it's become a grim joke. No election, and likely no mainstream political party, will answer the predicament of these 'marginal' groups. Yet they've come to this oven-like Kolkata in a defiant assertion of their existence and struggle, to hold this demonstration in the season of elections to remind the parties that they exist, they matter, and they are not going away; to remind us all that elections are, finally, about lives and livelihoods. Will they succeed in making a dent? Will they alter a single candidate's promise-making or post-election commitment? We'll see across the next month or so.

I notice a group of young tribals sitting with their drums. One of the drums is worn through, the black leather disc at the centre almost completely eaten away, and I have two contradictory thoughts. This is the Bengal that is connected by the eight-lane national highway of deprivation to other struggles in the country, to Kalinganagar in Orissa, to Jaitapur in Maharashtra, to Maheshwar in Madhya Pradesh. On the other hand, this is the immutable Bengali Resistance Gene, the one that has survived through the British Raj, the Congress years and the deadly CPM decades, and the one that will likely remain resilient through the tenure of whoever's coming next. I don't know how many years, if any, Trinamool will rule this state, but I notice the date and realize that an old drum, if not a bell, is already ringing on the current regime – as of today there are probably only thirty-four days left of the thirty-four years of Left rule in West Bengal.

11
APRIL

R-Day minus 32

Adda in Salt Lake

A couple of days later I find myself in a bar in the sterile precincts of soul-free Salt Lake, the vast agglomeration of bungalows, office buildings, pleasure parks and shopping malls that's grown like a hydrocele around the eastern edge of what used to be called 'Kolkata Proper'. The same friend, VR, has brought me to meet the Political Scientist who is one of the best analytical minds engaging with contemporary Bengali politics. Instead of immediately unfurling his *gyaan*, the PS is now interrogating my ignorance over a few whiskies. 'What do you think will happen now?' he asks me, popping a peanut into his mouth. 'I don't know,' I say feebly, thinking that he's stolen my question. 'I guess the Trinamool will come into some sort of power. They will try to do things for a bit. But after maybe about two years things will go back to how they were?'

As I try to expand on this, the PS interrupts me, his patience finally combusting. 'Listen,' he says, 'how can you say the old pattern will reimpose itself in two years' time? The one thing you have to understand is that, whoever comes to power, the old structure is now finished. Whether CPM comes back or, most likely, TMC takes over, the power management, the favour management, the bribery management, will all have to be different.' With little taps of his fingers between the bowls of mixture and ginger shreds in lime juice, the political gyaani lays out the future for me. Think not of the formations we see today: one street-fighting party, the CPM, ceding power to another one, the TMC – the only one who could challenge it, precisely because it's a spawn of the 'politics' perfected by the Left Front over three decades. Think instead of what happens two years hence, when the two different gangs of thieves start falling out internally. The Red gang because they've lost power and are under huge tectonic pressure, the Green gang because their ineptitude and venality in power is by now utterly exposed, the cracks inherent in their foundation now widening. Think also of the Congress sharks and BJP hyenas circling, smelling blood, both in the water and on land. Think of the different combinations this will throw up. Think of what kind of shopping mall Shonar Bangla will have become by then. Try and imagine these elections as a spectacular part of an irreversible chemical reaction and then try and imagine which elements and molecules will carrom into each other down time. It's going to be fascinating.

13

R-day minus 30

Songs of Bengal

'*Oder ke boledilam, aik thappod maarbo, kintu!*' I told them, I'll give you one slap! We are on the darkening highway, a few kilometres north of Krishnanagar, and suddenly, Mamata Banerjee is talking to me on my mobile. 'I am a political man!' she says. 'But why they are not understanding? I am also a simple man!'

As the voice shrills into my ear, I have to keep reminding myself I'm actually listening to one of the most brilliant mimics in this country and not Madam Railway Minister herself. The mimic is just fresh off having travelled in a car with Didi and she needs to share her excitement with me. 'She's something else, I tell you, just something else!' The mimic switches back to a normal voice. 'And I'm telling you, it's going to be a landslide!'

The connection from deep north Bengal is cut off, the mobile towers unable to withstand the high excitement, and the sound of the wind reoccupies my ears. But all the way till I reach Berhampore that night, the text messages keep hitting my phone from friends in the press who are following Didi and the other lady, who also leads a political party at the Centre. 'Amazing, massive show ... 1977 redux!', 'At meeting MB said same thing again, bt the crowd loves it!', 'Sonia here. Tomo Rahul cming. Plus Advani n Sushma for BJP. Wht an election this is turning out to be!'

Riding with me is a young press photographer, S, who's also working his phone, calling up reporters on the stump with MB and Sonia G to get a sense of what is happening. As the day's last meetings end and S's contacts finish filing, they start calling him back. Each time his phone rings, it emits the shard of Rabindra Sangeet that is its ring tone. A post-modern sound collage rapidly develops in the darkness of the van: *Keno chokher joley bhijiye diley na, shukno dhulo jawtoe-ooo...* 'Hello? Yes tell me, what did Mamata say? ... Right, right, okay, yes black money, the Left are like thieves themselves ... Listen, I'm getting another call so I'll call back. *Keno chokher joley bhijiye diley na* ... Yes, so, is Rahul actually coming tomorrow? Hanh? Uff, got cut off. *Why didn't you let me drench the dust with my tears* ... Hello, yes, so tomorrow, *pakka*? First meeting is where, Naxalbari? *Why didn't you let me drench the dust with my tears* ... 'So, okay, this guy just told me, first meeting is Naxlabari, 9 a.m., so when is he supposed to get to Farakka? What? 2.30? Okay. *Why didn't you let me drench the dust...*

I get the driver to stop at a roadside booze shop to pick up some fuel and the man offers me a clean, empty plastic bottle and some *minraal-bhotaar*. For the price of the whisky, the water and five extra bucks, he can mix the drink, making it easier to drink on the highway. I thank the man while declining the offer but I note that service philosophy in Bengal has clearly progressed since the last time I was on a highway here.

Moving on, I start talking to S about his collection of Rabindra Sangeet and he lays it out for me very proudly. He has several versions of different songs on his mobile phone. On his home computer, he has downloaded about 7GB of R-Sangeet, from which he replenishes his phone from time to time. Then there are the videos he has bookmarked on YouTube. In his off time, S, who is thirty-four years old, drives a Bullet and goes on long road trips, riding with friends in convoy. Many of them have Rabindra Sangeet as their preferred soundtrack. As our driver rides wave upon wave of oncoming high-beam truck headlights, S and I crack open the whisky, bump some of it into a half-filled bottle of mineral water and begin to knock it back. After a while, I get my first phone call of the evening, a contact calling from near Darjeeling. My ring tone happens to be the assassin boss's whistled tune from the movie *Kill Bill*.

The whistling is sharp enough to make S jerk his head in alarm, even though he's got on his headphones by now. I finish speaking and take a swig of whisky. I hand the plastic bottle to S who also takes a hit while looking at me with concern. Then, in a gesture of purest generosity, he pulls off his headphones and offers them to me. 'Dada, would you like to listen to my Rabindra Sangeet?' he asks. 'No, it's okay,' I say, but this only drives S to further effort, he's that kind of nice guy. 'I also have other music if you don't like Rabindra Sangeet, I can play that! Listen!' And he thumbs his keypad and brings up Mahmuduzzaman Babu singing '*Aaami Banglay gaan gaai, aami Banglar gaan gayi, ami amar amikey chirodin, ei Banglay khujey pai*'. I sing in Bengali, I sing the songs of Bengal, I find the me that's mine in this Bengal.

I listen, watching the roadside banana trees flicker by, silhouetted by the moon in this zone of the Twistes Tropiques.

I've not been on a night road in Bengal for about a decade now, and as we pass clusters of huts and the occasional townlet, I try and spot changes but I can't see anything looking different. The buildings themselves, along the main arterial highway north from Kolkata, still mostly seem to be of the same mud construction I've seen across the years. Electricity still seems to be an alien thing here, the few bulbs hanging in and around huts very, very dim. The road under our tyres is burred with constant bumping, only occasionally providing us with a smooth passage. From time to time, the van headlights sweep over election posters and party flags but even these look like they are remnants from some battle long ago. Driving through Bethuadahari, I see a statue of Gandhi in one corner of a *chowrasta*, the body slightly extra bent over, as if MKG is fielding at extra cover, and a bit later there's a lonely bust of I-Ganz lurking in the shadows. Crouching Gandhi, Hiding Indira.

We drive into Palashi with my friend Moushumi Bhowmick singing *'Aaami shunechhi shei din tumi shaagorer...'* I heard that you went to the sea that day. This Palashi is, I realize, the same Plassey where Robert Clive laid the bloody foundations of two hundred years of British rule on the subcontinent in 1757. Tonight, there is no sign that another momentous battle to rule Bengal is under way. We stop outside a roadside 'hoteyl' and park behind a new Indica with a Trinamool flag proudly attached to its nose. Inside the eatery, the young man who's the driver of the Indica is standing at the counter paying the bill. He has his striped T-shirt rolled all the way up under his armpits, displaying his curved and glistening torso to the world. His stomach pulsates with the food that's recently gone into it. He flips out the money with one hand while scratching his navel with the other. S watches with some disgust as the man gets into his Indica and drives off. 'We all want some kind of change,' he says softly, 'but the problem is, you see, *this* is their culture!'

'Is it so very different from the CPM's lumpen culture?' I ask. 'Aren't these the same guys who've been switching sides in small and big batches over the last few years?' I get no immediate reply from S who shakes his head in a 'yes but no' before turning his attention to the menu card.

In the bar in Salt Lake, the Political Scientist had laid it out for me: 'What are the three main things any new government will have to tackle here? One, the land issue. You can't say you want industry to prosper without working out some fair method of acquiring land from farmers. And after Nandigram and Singur that will now be difficult. Two, they will have to deal with the Maoists and the whole devastation of Junglemahal. Not easy. Third, equally importantly, they will have to do something about the para boys, the Boys' Club culture the CPM has fostered and which the Trinamool has used against the CPM so effectively. That is a huge, unemployed lumpen section, young men whose only job is to do whichever party's muscle work. What are you going to do about them?' Watching S's reaction to the guy with the midriff exhibition, I realize once again that this is the battleground, and it's not centred in any one place like Plassey-Palashi.

Later that night, when we reach our guest house in Berhampur, I'm put up in a room I'm told was occupied by Biman Bose two nights ago. Of the West Bengal CPM's head honchos that make up the Gang of Four, Bose is the oldest, sternest-looking and most austere. He is the ideologue who finally gives the 'party line' when tricky decisions have to be made. I look around the tube-lit room and imagine the Comrade settling down on the bed after a long day's campaigning. Before turning in myself, I go around the room and check carefully for any objects Bimanbabu might have left behind. I look in the empty bathroom, I look at the newly made beds, I make sure the balcony is empty. Finally, I check the ashtray for Navy Cut and bidi butts, but there are none. As I switch off the lights, I worry about my dreams bumping into residual traces of the Comrade's nightmares.

14
APRIL

Jumping Crow, Falling Mango

It is a properly hot mid-April day. The weather's been unusual so far but the summer's now clearly getting down to business. Across the day, the heat starts to meld different moments together.

Berhampur has a beautiful maidan surrounded by large old trees, a sizable square of green, clearly of Raj design, around which the British built their administration buildings. When I express surprise at the fact that the maidan has been preserved, my local guide snorts. 'It still belongs to the army. Otherwise the government would have definitely sold it off by now.' Among the official Raj bungalows and such others, is the police thana, also housed in a crumbling old structure with bluish-white lime flaking off the portico pillars. As we go inside to try and score our security passes, I'm hit

by the smell of ancient paper, solidified gum and dust. Passing the canyons of files, I'm suddenly transported back to 1977 and my days in Presidency College. The library of the college seemed not to have changed since the late nineteenth century and this police thana seems not to have changed since the Left came to power in 1977. In the office where they are making out the passes we are told we need further authorization from a 'Goumen Tophisaar'. So we head out again past the files and the already sleepy clerks.

Outside, a motley collection of cops mills about among the jam of parked police vehicles. Some of the men are in uniform, waving dormant walkie-talkies, some are in plain bush-shirts cradling ancient Sten guns and .303 Lee Enfields that look like they were last used in the Second World War. Everybody has an air of low-level excitement, a typical sense of slow-motion bustle that only uniformed Bengali officialdom generates. 'Which *gaadi* are we in? Bhai, I told you I wanted to be in that Sumo, didn't I?' And, even though it's barely past breakfast time: 'Have you counted the packed lunches? Make sure we don't fall short!' A cop is addressing a sleepy-looking black Labrador sniffer dog. 'Come on!' he says in English.

A slightly surreal sight awaits us in the SDO's office: as an audience of supplicants sits before the officer's desk, there are two men with cheap handicams, both standing on the same side of the room, videotaping proceedings. I wonder idly who is getting married. It takes me a while to understand that this is an EC monitoring team, there to record everything, banal or extraordinary, that happens during this special 'Election Time'. In the next few days, I will see many of these little cameras at work, creating a whole new surveillance archive for the delectation of future historians.

The presence of the commission is also very evident as we head to Farakka to catch Rahul Gandhi's meeting. On the highway we cross convoys of commandeered buses heading south to bring back paramilitary for the polling on the eighteenth. The country's most respected public institution, the EC, is choreographing the country's least respected one, the 'puuleesh', for a special dance in this Carnival of Equality.

Nearing the meeting ground, we start getting updates. 'Rahul's running late. The meeting in Naxalbari was supposed to be at nine-thirty and he still hadn't arrived at ten.' Then, a few minutes later, 'He did Naxalbari but only spoke for seven minutes!'

At the ground there are SPG in grey safari suits everywhere, walking through a muted rainbow of other uniforms like lions padding through lesser, inedible animals. The BJP has put up pictures of their candidate Hemanta Ghosh right next to Rahul Gandhi's, so that R-baba will see them when he drives past. As the Safaris watch the police watching the people, the EC marriage-video boys are there too, filming everything.

Just outside the bamboo enclosures for the meeting, a mini-road bazaar has set up, selling *ghugni*, ice cream, tea, cucumbers. The cucumber man has lined his trolley with newspapers and an odd typeface catches my eye. A Gujarati newspaper – the *Sorath Bhaskar* from Rajkot. My guide is unsurprised. 'A lot of labour goes from here to Gujarat, masons, jewellery workers, factory workers. Constant coming and going.'

When the ice-cream man hears that I'm doing a series on the elections he switches on his sound-byte machine, pithy and articulate: 'Whoever wins, the man who today has two wheels will not get to own four wheels. He may get another set of two wheels but he won't get to four wheels. So what difference does it make?'

In the far background behind the bamboo podium covered with tricolour cloth looms the NTPC power plant with its huge chimneys. The press *biradari* huddles in the shade of the solitary mango tree in the maze of bamboo pens put up for the anticipated crowd. As the two-wheel and no-wheel people start to trickle in, the Big-wheel baba goes off the radar. One by one, the reporters and photographers' phones start buzzing. 'Massive storm around Siliguri.' 'Rahul's chopper is lost!' 'It's been found!' 'He has been diverted!' 'Impossible flying weather, he's gone back to Delhi!' In the middle of all this a violent dust storm encases us. The NTPC chimneys disappear from sight. A veteran photographer sniffs the air and says, 'I can smell Rahul's chopper on this wind!' Somebody gives us detail: 'He'll drive to Purnea and take another chopper from there, go around the storm in Siliguri to come here.' The trees at the edge of the ground shake in the fierce wind and a bright green hailstorm hits the ground: baby mangoes become pebbles smacking down from the branches, and kids run around collecting them. A couple of goats, unbothered by the dust storm, indulge in flagrant, procreative *oposhonshkriti*. Clearly, they too see a bright future post the departure of the Red Prudes. The wind dies down and the heat returns like an old tyrant recapturing power. On the PA system, someone stops the wail of *'Ai Mere Vatan ke Logon'* and replaces it with a long modern riff on *'Vande Mataram'*.

By 4 p.m., a boisterous crowd is in and the speeches have begun. *'Kongreshpaati maanush ke shongey niye choley.'* The Congress takes people along with it. *'Ei oppodartho shorkar ke baar korun!'* Get rid of this useless government. The legendary Ghani Khan's brother repeats everything in threes: *'Congress ke bhote din, bhote din, bhote din! CPM ke harabo, harabo, harabo!'* Vote for the Congress, we will defeat the CPM. All the Bangla speakers sound slightly drunk but it's probably just the accent around here in Murshidabad-Malda. Suddenly the veteran photographer takes his eye away from his tele-lens. *'Jaah, o aashchhey na! Daikh, SPG palacchey!'* He's not coming, look, the SPG is scarpering. Behind the podium, the safari suits have begun to evacuate quietly, pulling their wheeled suitcases across the bumpy ground.

Sure enough, Adhir Chowdhury, local Congress maverick, comes on and announces in a sonorous, sorrowful, crocodile voice: 'It fills me with as much sadness as it does you, but I've just been told by the DIG of the SPG that Rahul Gandhi will not be coming to Farakka today.' Parts of the crowd begin to disperse immediately, young men touching the guy in front lightly on the back, low urgency, not yet ready to push. Suddenly, all the no-go areas are accessible to us, clearly no one poses any threat to these local politicians. 'What? Are you leaving just because Rahul's not coming?' I ask a group of boys as they jog out of the mango orchard. 'Exactly! We see these people day in and day out, but we wanted to see Rahul!'

An old Kolkata acronym we used in the 1970s comes to mind: Kaak Laphaalo but Paankh Down, KLPD. Living in Delhi, Rahul Gandhi would only have heard the far cruder version used by students of JNU and Delhi U, but the meaning is the same: having the high anticipation of something dashed at the last minute.

Someone on the podium is going on about how a *kaal-boishaakhi jhor* will sweep away the CPM but the only storm visible now is the dust from the people leaving. For a while, the field becomes like a history of the Congress party filmed by the Hungarian master Miklos Jansco: crowds of people moving away even as snakes of new processions arrive, shouting slogans, still in single file, unaware as yet that their hero is standing them up. Hiding Indira, Missing Rahul. We don't know it then, but R-baba will hit each and every one of his scheduled meetings from Naxalbari in the morning (7 minutes) to Mothabari in the evening (12 minutes), missing out only on Farakka and the five-thousand-odd people gathered there.

That evening, I sit on the bed vacated by Biman Bose, having a drink with S and a couple of other journalists. All of them are now convinced that Rahul never intended to stop at Farakka. 'Did you see how easily the SPG let us through? If someone with Z security was really coming, Manmohan, Sonia, Rahul, they would have taken apart every camera, made you take off the lens, made you fire the shutter. They did none of that. They knew this was a dummy meeting.' Another journo has doubts. 'Maybe, maybe not. Their choppers don't fly in storms and there was a storm, so clearly he had to choose which place to miss. I think it was more likely a snub to Adhir for disobeying high command orders and putting up candidates against the Trinamool.' Across the chatter I realize Rahul Gandhi was just an extra treat for voters already in the Congress bag. Whatever the reason for Rahul bypassing Farakka, nobody imagines today's KLPD will make any difference to the vote.

15

R-Day minus 28

Scrawny Little State

'Who cares about your scrawny little state and what happens in the elections there?' My friend is calling from Delhi and I can sort of see his point. As I speak to him, I'm actually on the road in the scrawny neck of West Bengal, where the territory gets squeezed between Bihar and Bangladesh, and, looking around me, I can see what my friend means. The road from Malda that connects to NH 34 heading north isn't exactly bad, Malda city isn't exactly a dump, the Farakka Barrage we've crossed a little while back isn't exactly falling apart, but there's something slightly askew about all of it.

My irritation has actually begun early that morning while leaving Berhampur. Having said my goodbyes to S and the others, I managed an early enough departure but the driver stopped at a petrol station to fill up before starting the long drive. He efficiently opened the cap of the tank for the attendant. The fuel came through the pipe and nozzle at a speed comparable to anywhere in India. The numbers on the digital counters flickered as they do elsewhere in the country. My driver shut the cap and asked for the bill. Fifteen minutes later, I was still at the petrol station, standing on the road just outside, puffing on an unscheduled cigarette. In the time we'd been there, the station was visited by one other vehicle, a solitary motorcycle. The attendant, a nice quiet man in his fifties, took a full ten minutes to find his bill-pad. I didn't realize it then, because he said nothing to me or my driver, but the next delay had to do with finding a working pen. An operation that should take no more than seven minutes took nearly thirty. The worst thing is, at no point did the nice attendant show any sense of urgency or contrition – he had no clue he was wasting our time, this is just how things were.

Heading back north past the mango orchard of Rahul Gandhi's non-meeting, I saw that workers had nearly finished dismantling the podium. It wasn't even 8 a.m. and this efficiency was unusual – no doubt the bamboo and tricolour bunting were in hot demand elsewhere in this busy season. We stopped at a dhaba just short of Farakka to have breakfast. Scattered around the charpais were CRPF soldiers also on their way up to the northern districts for Phase 1. I liked the way one group had piled their sub-machine guns in the centre of a charpai as they ate around the weaponry. As I reached for my camera, something made me stop. Perhaps it was better to ask for permission before some jawan with pickle on his fingers got trigger-happy. I looked around and spotted the CO, a short, truculent-looking Sardarji. 'Good morning, sir. I'm from the press. Can I take a photo of your men eating?' I realized the taller guy next to Surdy was an officer of even higher rank. Surdy managed to look even more unamused than he was earlier. 'No. Photos only when we are on the road.' Telling myself there was no immediately visible human-rights abuse going on, I backed off.

In a little while we were crawling along in the speed-restricted traffic on the top of the Farakka Barrage. The barrage is a Central government concern, and the steel curtains that choreograph the massive water-flow seemed to be in good shape, but the decayed concrete of the railings along the carriageway and the torpor of the paramilitary guards seemed, somehow, to be purely Waste-Bungle. I looked at the body of water flowing away and suddenly I felt I was at a nodal point: Darjeeling to the north, Bihar just to the west, Nadia and Murshidabad to the south, and all of vast Bangladesh to the east.

Malda is a busy, overgrown little town and it's only when we reached there did I realize today was *Poila Boishaakh*, Bengali New Year's day. All around us loudspeakers blared music, the kids' exams be damned, and many shops were distributing *sandesh* and flowers. I needed to find a road map of the state to replace the one I'd left behind at the guest house. All I was offered, in shop after book-and-stationery shop, was a schoolchild's outline map, the thin squiggly black line encircling a blank space – fill in your own fantasy of the state here, reality is irrelevant. Clearly, not many people in Malda needed to check where they were or what lay around them. It's equally a failing of insular Kolkatans like myself, but today I found this trait especially annoying.

But by the time we make our (mapless) way on to National Highway 34, I'm feeling a lot better. Looking around as the speedometer crosses 120 kmph, I can fool myself that we are in Haryana or Punjab. We left Malda's famous mango orchards behind in the morning. Now, as we approach Siliguri, the outriders of tea bushes start running alongside.

I haven't been to Siliguri for a while. Driving into the outskirts I'm slightly shocked at the new buildings, the shopping mall and the press of traffic on the roads. After the small-town feel of Berhampur ('This is our famous sweet shop where Pranab-babu and Rahul ate sandesh during the 2009 Lok Sabha elections'), Siliguri feels like a modern version of a Klondike gold rush 'city' that's been quickly put up. I've only been away from Kolkata for two days but coming back into a proper urban space is a jolt. By the time we pull up to the hotel, the smoke, the neon signs, the motorcycle showrooms and the modern hotel boxes, five, six, seven storeys high, have let me know I've reached a burgeoning urban conglomeration of the twenty-first century.

My contact in Siliguri is precise about what's been happening. Mamata has won over people here. She has said to the business class, 'We are not unaware that you are Bengal's most important commercial city after Kolkata.' Earlier, in 2009, the westernized college kids ignored Trinamool. No longer. This time MB's rallies have drawn college girls who have clearly become fans. The Trinamool Congress is at least set to squeak past the CPM, if not sweep the polls. The Star Ananda–Neilsen poll headlining *The Telegraph* this morning has no such marginal projections. Their calculations are telling them the Trinamool Alliance is on course to win 215 seats, with the Left being reduced to rubble with a mere 74 MLAs.

'Who cares what happens to your scrawny little Bengal?' My friend had asked earlier in the day. As I turn in after the long drive, a kind of answer starts to play in my head: think of West Bengal as a pressure cooker on low heat containing ninety million people. Think of the Left Front as the lid with a faulty valve which hasn't allowed steam to escape for about twenty years. Think of MamBan as the cook who's just about to pry open the lid. Think of what will boil over, what will randomly singe the hand that lifts the lid, think of the slow, dark, lethal fermentation that's been cooking inside all this while. Think not of the old adage that is now a joke – 'What Bengal thinks today, India thinks tomorrow' – but more, perhaps, that what Bengal has been through over the last two decades may be a harbinger of what other parts of India may go through over the next decade. Think of Mumbai and Bangalore already sliding towards Kolkatafication, think of the UP highway protests as spawned by Singur and Nandigram, think of what will happen when the pressure-cooker lids are lifted off long-maintained political cultures of violence and fear, whether secular or Hindutva, whether party-centric or family-centric. Remember what may have taken twenty to thirty years to become fully ripened abscesses in slow-moving Bengal might not take half that long in other parts of the country. No matter whether MamBan is successful, middling or a complete disaster as a chief minister, think that this is why the rest of the country needs to pay attention to scrawny West Bengal, to its tragic past and its possibly thorny future.

R-Day minus 27

Partially Occluded Area

'For the stupid, bloody Bangali bhadralok these people have always been *darwans* and nothing else.' I've bumped into a friend from Kolkata and we are standing on the balcony of the Planters' Club in Darjeeling. My friend is a classic Kolkata bhadralok himself and his cold-eyed fury is articulate and passionate, as only the best of his class can produce. 'I mean, just look at this place! Look what's happened to it!'

We're looking down at Keventer's and the boat-shaped bar that some mini-tsunami of entrepreneurship has recently flung on top of the building across the lane. 'Talk about neglect! Of course people here want Gorkhaland, why wouldn't they? The only reason there's still some charm and some preservation of the environment is because, all these years, the CPM couldn't get its act together to come north and ruin

this area. Otherwise, there's nothing here for these people, you can see the place is falling apart.'

I've been seeing since the previous day, when I left Siliguri early in the morning and took the winding road up. After climbing for a while, when you look out through the car window, you get slight vertigo. Through the gaps in the stands of tall trees you can see all of blue Bengal stretching away below. As you go higher, nature switches on the air conditioner and puts the setting to just a little cooler than you want it. After Kurseong it's definitely sweater time, as you wind through mist and back into sunlight. Accompanying us is the track of the toy train, cutting in and out across the road like some ancient 3D game of snakes and ladders installed by long-dead giants. Every few kilometres there are women crouching on the inside of the road, holding plastic canisters to the mouths of

pipes coming down the rock face. The pipes emit only thin dribbles of water. In the lush greenery and the mist we are surrounded by moisture, but translating it to usable water seems to be an arduous task. Further up, there are kids playing cricket on the road, game after game with plastic canisters now serving as wickets, planks for bats and rags rolled and tied together for balls. Someone Dhonies a shot across a descending Eicher truck and the 'ball' goes over the cliff; it's now the batsman's turn to get Dhonied by the other boys. Somewhere near Ghum, driving through a small town, the toy train finally scrapes past us, looking no more elegant than a very small and dilapidated Kolkata tram. As we get closer to Darjeeling, the density of habitation increases and it doesn't take much to imagine the city of Darjopolis starting more or less from Kurseong in twenty years' time, all the houses clinging to the road

while behind them lies the devastation of one of the most beautiful tracts of nature in the world.

The Planters' Club is lovely, old world, and yet another splintering icon of the rough-hewn pine and teak pomp of the old Raj-era tea culture. The building itself still has a nice façade and decent enough innards but now the club and its neighbour, Keventer's ('Kev's' in the new parlance), are surrounded by the bustling tawdriness of T-shirt stalls and the smoke and noise of far too many mountain-killing four-wheeled vehicles. The afternoon I get there is the last day of electioneering in the district and the campaigns are clearly having a last blast before closing. On this unseasonally overcast day, the loudspeaker speeches bounce across the valley in sawing echoes. The voices are unclear, and I don't speak Nepali anyway, but there seems to be a very hoarse anger here. Not the jatra outrage of normal Bangla political *boktita* but a very real, barely pent-up rage.

The demand for a separate Gorkha political identity stretches as far back as 1907, I'm told. Under the British, the region came under Bihar for a time and – so a story goes – on 14 August 1947 a Pakistan flag was hoisted on the clock tower before the Indians corrected the mistake and assigned the tea paradise to West Bengal. British, Bihari, East Pakistani and Bengali, none of these labels took any notice of Gorkha identity or aspirations, or so goes the argument.

'We only have three MLAs here, but the trouble the area causes for Kolkata and the CM of West Bengal is as if we had thirty!' says one local young journalist.

This is what is known as a 'Partially Excluded Area' where all the Republic's rules do not apply, or not necessarily in the same way they do in the plains. I suspect it could also be called a 'Partially Occluded Area': what the tourists and the tea merchants don't see as they pass through is that this is a different zone from the rest of Bengal, not just geographically but also in terms of its society. It's in the attempt to have the right to represent and define this zone, this culture, that three important parties are slugging it out for the three hill seats in these Assembly elections. The CPM and Congress are in it too, but they are minor players in the local battle, and the Tinno people don't yet have the spread to put up candidates here.

Small, moss-drenched guest houses, obscure temples and 'educational institutes', shops and eateries curl inwards against the morning that has now turned fully grey and damp. If I thought Pranab Mukherjee lived in an ugly three-storey, the Darjeeling residence Subash Ghisingh has recently fought to reoccupy is even uglier, a brown-grey, unpainted, four-storey concrete bunker at the curve of a steep road. There's no crowd in front of the house, no fleet of SUVs to mark it out as the house of a big political leader. What is in place, however, is a small scattering of serious-looking men hanging around outside, two men staring from behind a low wall at a vantage point, and a tall, locked gate. There are four or five men crowded behind the gate, including one armed khaki uniform. Every time someone authorized to enter approaches the gate, the doorkeeper laboriously opens the big padlock and lets them in, before carefully and ostentatiously locking up again. Every time someone leaves, the same routine is followed. Ghisingh, who many wrote off as a political has-been, has made a recent comeback into Hill politics but it's not clear which enemies might warrant such extreme caution.

I send my request through the gate: writing special election diary for *The Telegraph*, would like to meet Ghisingh-ji for a brief while. We wait. People come and go. The lock clearly needs some slight oiling but I suspect the people sitting around find the squeak comforting. A man comes to the gate and asks again about my provenance and identity. The reply is translated to him and he goes away. Another man starts talking to the two of us who are waiting – rapid, serious, confident. He is a follower of Ghisingh but perhaps not in the innermost circle, given that he's loitering outside the locked gate. 'We're taking Darjeeling and Kurseong tomorrow,' he informs us. We nod in non-disagreement. A really tiny man carrying an overflowing satchel hurries up to the gate and is immediately let in. I'm informed he's Ghisingh's trusted photographer, the one whom Ghisingh asks to record all the important events of his struggle. A sudden swirl of mist passes between people and I idly wonder if it's a smoke grenade preceding some deadly Gorkha-ninja attack. As if to punish me for such thoughts, the man returns to the gate and says the Leader can only meet me tomorrow, long after I planned to leave.

Back down in the main town, I meet Bharati Tamang, whose husband Madan Tamang, the leader of the Akhil Bharatiya Gorkha League, was killed last May right in front of the Planters' Club. She is standing on the street before her party office. She and another younger woman lead us into the plain two-room office where some chairs are vacated near a desk. 'Ei! Halla kamti!' Pipe down! someone calls to the workers gathered in the front room. Mrs Tamang sits down next to Laxman Pradhan who answers most of the questions. Later, when I talk to a local woman who will vote tomorrow, she tells me, 'Bharati Tamang is a very nice lady but she is only in politics to get justice for the murder of her husband.' Mrs Tamang and Laxman Pradhan are flanked by Sushma Ghosh-Gurung who's a teacher in a local college, and a veteran of the party, Mohan Thapa.

The primary issues for the League are thus: a 'long-term settlement for the region', law and order after the end of the election's Code of Conduct period the day after tomorrow, i.e., the fear of attacks on them by the Morcha, and justice for the murder of Madan Tamang. To this they also add the business of the water-shortage and the embezzlement of government funds by officials hand-in-glove with the other party. Last but not least on their shopping list is the establishment of 'true democracy in the area'.

'Whatever protection you give a citizen of Kolkata, you must give the same protection to a citizen of Darjeeling,' Bharati Tamang says, not unreasonably.

We go through the routine of what will happen tomorrow, the polling booths, the lists, the polling

agents and their job, the moving of the machines to a strongroom in North Point School. At some point old man Mohan Thapa takes off about how they were defrauded in 1999 and how he can never trust these vote boxes again. The others tell him the button machines are actually okay. 'No. Every button might give you the same result!' Thapa insists, and I can see the others accepting defeat.

Leaving the office, I get a real sense that these people are not expecting to win anything tomorrow. If they give the Morcha a serious run for a couple of the seats and if they don't lose their deposit in the others, it will have been a good election for them.

Across Darjeeling, at the headquarters of the Morcha in Singamari, there is no such shyness. Roshan Giri, general secretary and No.2 of the Morcha, leans back and ends the discussion before I can begin it. 'We have won the election. We won it when we declared our candidates.' He proffers us a plate of excellent hot momos. I try and ask him difficult questions such as: 'You've promised people Gorkhaland. What will happen if you can't keep that promise?' He shrugs, he looks at his Blackberry, he smiles at me indulgently like a Gujju billionaire who has just bought out the local paan-walla. 'We will struggle. Gorkhaland will come. It has to.' Translated, it means, 'Don't ask silly questions. Remove your belongings. Tomorrow, I'm starting to build the factory here.'

After a few minutes of this relaxed and affable exchange ('Have some tea. Though you shouldn't have tea so

soon after momos, it's not a good combination!'),
he and Dawa Lama, the treasurer, who's been sitting
quietly and smiling, are joined by Trilok Dewan, the
Morcha candidate for Darjeeling. I turn to Dewan,
asking him what he plans to do tomorrow. 'Oh, I will
move around,' he says, also affably.

In the face of such warm confidence, I run out of
questions. Dewan decides to help me out. 'Actually, we
are just the racehorses,' says the former chief secretary
of Andhra Pradesh, humbly pointing to Dawa Lama.
'These people are the jockeys telling us where to go!'
Lama, who obviously has a sense of humour, raises
his eyebrows and offers me more momos to go with
my tea.

17

R-Day minus 26

Kaalboishaakhi

Early the next morning, I begin my journey back south. As our van winds its way through the streets of Darjeeling, I see clusters of people, small queues already forming near the voting booths, paramilitary at regular intervals, looking bored but wide awake. On the hill road down, the scene repeats itself, small groups of people, occasionally a desk in the awning of a shop where the different party volunteers have set up camp, more soldiers, their sub-machine guns making them look like overdressed guests at a casual picnic.

Reaching Siliguri, I meet my reporter contact and he tells me the most exciting news is that two or three of the automatic voting machines have broken down, holding up the polling at the booths. There is, it seems, none of the violence that usually herds crowds away from polling stations.

As we drive out of Siliguri back on to NH 34, I wonder what MamBan will do with this area if and when she comes to power. She's not a bhadralok and she probably doesn't see the Gorkhas as darwans, but MB has all the makings of a champion jockey: arrogance, daring, the short height. Sitting in the saddle, I wonder how she will deal with all these fast and erratic hill thoroughbreds I've just met.

By mid-afternoon we are back in the squiggly neck of Bengal and the heat outside our motorized AC bubble is strong enough to make one forget that the highest mountains in the world are a less than a hundred kilometres away. My pal from Delhi catches me on my mobile between Dalkhola and Malda at almost the same spot he called me two days ago.

'Listen. What's it looking like? I've got a friend here, long-time CPM fellow-traveller, who's saying the party's confident there will be a last-minute pro-Left wave once people realize they are about to give Mamata a free ride into power. He's saying the CPM's internal reports are telling them they will be hit badly but they will hang on to power with a wafer-thin majority.'

I suddenly find myself irritated at all the Lefty fellow-travellers sitting on the lawns under Delhi's April blossoms. 'The only wafer is going to be up their ass,' I reply, 'and that wafer's not going to be particularly thin, okay?'

Unfazed by my reply, my friend goes through the calculations given to him by the fellow-traveller. 'So, majority is something like 148 out of 294, right? My comrade friend here is claiming the Left Front will manage about 150 and then get a couple of Independents to join them. So, 152–153. Says it will be tough but they will hold on to power.'

'Are they planning to cosy up to the BJP, by any chance? You know, like, orange underpants under red pyjamas? What?'

'No ... he says they think they can actually do it without the BJP's two-and-a-half seats or whatever.'

I don't see it, but I'm not a psephologist, pollster or any other kind of political soothsayer, so I leave my friend with a return barb: 'In any case, all of you are clearly hooked by what's going to happen in this scrawny little state, aren't you?'

The steam-cooker of an afternoon stays with us till we reach Farakka, but as we cross the barrage, clouds magically begin to darken the sky. By the time I reach my hotel in Berhampur, there is a proper kaalboishaakhi gale shaking the lighter mopeds and scooters lined up in the parking lot for somebody's wedding reception. My local guide is waiting for me in the lobby, having arranged my booking. He agrees to have a quick drink in my room before heading home for his dinner. We aren't halfway through the drink before the rain starts to smash down and it becomes clear my friend isn't leaving any time very soon.

Over the next hour the only subject of discussion are the elections. Being someone who's followed several elections, my man lays it all out for me. 'You know, I've done the sums and I can't really see the Baamphront getting less than a 100 seats. Here's how.' The man goes through the state district by district, locality by locality, ticking off unassailable LF seats, marginal seats and sure-fire Tinno-Congress wins. Outside, the rain manages to bend the lone pine tree in the hotel courtyard like a bow. At the end of the calculation he agrees with himself, with no argument from me, that the Left should get anything between 100 to 120 seats.

'That would be ideal,' I say.

'Yes. Exactly. Because it would be a disaster if they somehow manage to win.'

'And if they get less than a hundred ...'

'That too, would be terrible.' The man is about my age and he knows all too well the effects unbridled power

can have upon a political party. 'Can you imagine if these people come in with 215-230 like the poll is predicting?'

'Yes.'

'They will roll over everything. The Baamphront will have to hide!'

The next morning, just before I reach Krishnanagar, I see the first sign in days that the Left has not yet gone into hiding. A long CPM bike rally passes us, going in the other direction. Some older men but mostly youngsters, schoolboys and men in their early twenties, red flags flicking in the handlebars. They notice my camera poking out of the van window and break into lusty shouts. *'In-klub! Jeinyaabbad! In-klub, jeinyaabbad!'*

Passing through the glass canyons of Rajarhat, or what I call 'Gurgaon East', I see a sign with some letters missing: *'yot Bas Nagar'.* It's only a little over a year since Jyoti Basu died and the quick dilapidation of something named after him seems to be a harbinger of some sort. In terms of a badly stretched pun, it's even worse: 'yot' is close to 'jote', the Bangla word for 'alliance' that's being attached to the Tinno-Cong-I side, and 'bas' is 'home' or 'domicile'. If you were to be reading the runes and coffee grains, the sign could easily be saying 'Jote Baash Nogor': this is the town where the Alliance resides.

R-Day minus 22

A Few Small Mistakes

The crowd spots their Leader and a great roar goes up. The Leader waves and nods, approving the crowd's passion. The crowd responds to the great man's approval and roars again. The Leader waves again, and points over their heads, turning his followers' attention to the struggle at hand. Some of the people obey, others are glued to their raised mobiles, capturing grainy pictures of The Leader who's standing so unbelievably close. A mother of two teenagers can't decide whether to use her mobile to photograph or talk. Finally, the excitement of conveying her proximity to Greatness wins over the need to get yet another tiny photo. She touches herself as she burbles into the phone. '*Haan, o thik eikhaaney daadiye achhey! Amaader thik opore! Aarey, tui bishhash korchhish na, ki bolbo! Just amader oporer stand-ey!*' Yes, He's standing just here, just right above us, you don't believe me but in the stand just above us. *'Haan, daikh, TV tey daikh, Gauri o acchey! Oph-shouldaar dress!'* Yes, Gauri is also there, look at the TV, off-shoulder dress!

Gautam Gambhir hammers a shot, one bounce across the boundary. The pre-recorded trumpet-command blares out on the loudspeakers and the crowd erupts, 'Kay-Kay-Aar! Kay-Kay-Aar!' The six cheerleader stands develop tiny cyclones of blonde hair as the girls wave their pompoms and celebrate a sure victory for the Knight Riders. People finish cheering and once again turn their backs to the game, to continue with the main business of the evening – waving at Shah Rukh Khan and trying to catch his eye. SRK's eyes, however, are obscured by shades and his face is impassive. But he raises a soft fist and pumps it, softly, approving of Gambhir's shot. He blows a kiss to the constituency. He gyrates, gently, to the music that blares out between overs. The crowd around his box-balcony goes crazy.

Around us, Eden Gardens looks resplendent, like a bride that's missed the bus to her own wedding, but who's doing just fine at someone else's post-*shaadi* bash. The clouds are darkening the dusk sky above the bright lights and that adds to the contrast of the picture-postcard scene: the purple and gold pennants, the swooping boom-cam, the big screens on the sides and the shouting whooping crowd that's filled almost three-fourths of the stadium. Around me, there are a few rows of empty seats being jealously guarded by a black-white mama; it's unlikely any claimants will now appear, ten overs into the forty, but he's not a Kolkata cop for nothing, and he isn't about to give up his beautiful patch of plastic buckets – diligently, he shoos away anyone trying to slide in for a better view, either of Shah Rukh or of the game.

The previous night, I was at another great Kolkata institution just a few yards away from the stadium. The Town Hall next to the High Court is a grand, august pile, and upon entering it one wonders why the place doesn't feature more often in public events of the city. On the night before the KKR-Bangalore game, I'm here for *The Telegraph*/CNN-IBN T-20 between the Tinommul Tomcats and the Maakshish Mohishasurs. Labelled 'The Battle for Bengal', the debate is being hosted by Rajdeep Sardesai. Gloved up on the T-mul side is Derek O'Brien, dancing on his toes, wearing a fine, almost see-through, white kurta. Squaring up in the Red corner is a young contender in the shape of a very dapper and corporate looking Prosenjit Bose, who heads the CPM's Research Cell in the distant provincial town of New Delhi.

The debate begins with Sardesai asking Bose to explain why voters should give the Left Front another five years. Puncher Prosenjit tries to say too much too quickly, manages to say nothing very much and ends with an admission of mistakes, leaving his jaw open for a quick counterpunch from Bruiser O'Brien: 'He had two minutes to explain three decades and he began well by admitting they've made loads and loads of mistakes!' And then the floodgates open, one by one, questions about the problems of Left Front rule start to pop up from the audience and Puncher is reeling.

Back at Eden, the next day, Yusuf Pathan delivers some mighty blows for KKR, managing to bring up what looks like a fighting total. Chris Gayle gets rid of Pathan with a blinder of a reaction catch at short cover but no matter, the crowd is delirious. SRK and his shades both look happy as he disappears behind the glass doors of his box for the break. Unlike at the Town Hall, it looks like there's a game on.

Surprisingly, the problems for Bruiser O'Brien start pretty early too. It's not as if Puncher Prosen is managing to hit the ribs or anything, but the audience is doing it for him, a bit like those side-wrestlers in WWF who jump over the ropes behind a main contestant to hit him on the back of the head. Sure the Left Front is bad, but who has faith in your ragtag bunch of overaggressive neophytes? No one. Look at your record in Kolkata Corporation. Look at what the Tinno unions have done in the colleges! How can we have faith?

'So!' asks Rajdeep, happy to feel his feet slipping in the blood of both fighters. 'So, is Bengal between the Devil and the Deep Blue Sea? We will find out after the break!'

After the innings break at Eden, the expectant crowd sits down with snacks, waiting for their dessert of Bangalore wickets. After an over or so, there is action right next to me, typically Kolkata/Bengal action. An officer dresses down a cowering young khaki home guard and snatches away his mobile phone. He turns to two other hapless khaki cops and screams at them: *'Tomader ke post chhedey eikhaane aashtey ke bolechhilo?'* Who asked you to leave your post and come here? The three have clearly sidled into the empty seats to catch a look at … HIM. Looks like it's at least going to cost one of them the phone with which he was taking pictures. *'JAAO!'* Go! the officer screams and the three boys scurry back to their posts. The black-white mama looks satisfied at having his empty seats returned to him.

Chris Gayle takes this as a signal to switch on the drum-machine he clearly forgot to bring along from Jamaica the last three years when he was in KKR colours. *Boom. Boom. Pum-pum … Boom.* A sparse melody of singles and twos is suddenly underlaid by the pumping, unrelenting riddim 'n' base of sixes and fours. Kolkata's famously sporting, cricket aficionado crowd goes deathly silent.

At the Town Hall, under the high Doric pillars with their peeling white plaster, the one-sided match has now become far more even. Sardesai is moving from student to young student as they express their frustration at the many mini-fascisms of the Mohishasurs, he holds the mike to a high-school boy who says, 'We are caught between megalomaniacs and a madwoman.'

Back at Eden, as Gayle finishes stomping on his former team, SRK's shades come off. Maybe the dark circles under his eyes are an illusion formed by the banks of bright Eden lights. He doesn't see the boy but there he is, one teenage worshipper, big-bottomed, dark-skinned, light-eyed, who keeps swaying even when the music has gone off, hoping the Man will look at him.

At the Town Hall, O'Brien objects to the description of 'madwoman', asking the young man not to get personal. I silently agree. Whatever else she may be, Mamata Banerjee is the least mad person in this state. Besides, if things go wrong for the T-mul, whether in thirty-four weeks or thirty-four months, I don't want anyone of her party to be able to hide behind that epithet of 'mad'. Puncher Prosen then produces the line of the evening. Defending the Left Front's rule, he says, 'Yes, we have some small mistakes.' Bruiser jumps on this like Chris Gayle on a slow full-toss. 'Did you *hear* him? He said *a-few-small* mistakes!'

Prosenjit asks a final return question to which Derek O'Brien once again replies, 'I don't have to answer any questions from you!' As Sardesai winds up, I think of the best point made this evening, which is by *The Telegraph*'s Manini Chatterjee when she points out that it's high time these two parties began to develop a more civil, less vicious, culture of debate and political competition for the sake of the people of the state. I check the calendar and think Bruiser O'Brien has perhaps only a few weeks left during which he can refuse to answer questions from the Opposition.

22
APRIL

R-Day minus 22

A Big Mistake

On 22 April, Anil Basu, the veteran CPM leader, makes a speech at his former parliamentary constituency, Arambagh. At one point Basu raises his arms and shouts *'Ora boley Mamata maaney shototaa!'* They say Mamata means integrity! He then spreads his fingers in a claw and moves his hand and pelvis in a thrusting rhythm. *'Mamata … shotota! Mamata … shotota! KISHER shotota?'* What integrity? 'She said in Haora, "I have been offered money from Bangalore and Chennai, but I have not taken it." Absolutely correct! Why should she take money from Bangalore or Chennai? When a whore in Sonagachhi gets a big client, she has no time for smaller babus!' Another thrust of the revolutionary pelvis, another obscene clawing gesture from the hand. *'America* is in there now! So why should she take money from Bangalore and Chennai?' Basu is wearing the classical Bengali CPM uniform when he says this,

sweat-crumpled dhoti-kurta, which is also the costume in which the babus visiting the red-light district of Sonagachhi have been typically portrayed in Bengali cinema and theatre. Masturbating the air with his hand, Basu leaves nothing to the imagination. He also leaves an indelible image of a cheap, dirty old man in the minds of viewers across the state. The image also inevitably connects to the attacks CPM's goons have carried out on women across the decades, Bantolla and Birati, where women were forced to walk naked while others were raped and murdered, and more recently Nandigram, where women were gang-raped.

What is lost in the outrage is that MamBan is no slouch herself in the street-slanging department. With all the overload of cricket around, an analogy comes to mind. With all her screaming and addressing the CPM as 'tui' and 'I'll give them one slap!', MB and the Tinno people could be compared to the kind of overaggressive bowler fielding off his own bowling, who pretends to take a shy at the stumps while actually aiming for the batsman who's well within his crease. Basu's retaliation could then be compared to a throw-ball beamer, aiming for the batsman's head.

In any case, all hell breaks loose and Buddhadeb Bhattacharya is forced to censure Basu and order him off the party's campaign programme. The Tinno unsurprisingly milk the outrage for all it's worth. A senior journalist friend shakes his head as we watch the Anil Basu clip on YouTube. 'This fucker's just cost the CPM a couple of lakh votes!'

24
APRIL

R-Day minus 20

Why be Afraid of Red?

The red songs of Revolution ring out across the evening meeting. The group on the stage are good, disciplined voices, perfectly modulated yet passionate. A harmonium, four women in chorus, two men on either side with clear high throats singing about the mountain of fire – the anger – that has built up against oppression. The audience is seated on plastic chairs, quiet, alert, made up of all ages, but not that many youngsters. Outside the perimeter of the *maathh*, a crowd stands watching. In the low buildings around, a few people in the windows and on the terraces. A news cameraman pans over the meeting, singing along with the troupe, the words clearly like the lullaby sung to him as a baby. After a while, the singers change over and an older man comes to the mike. This time the tune is a traditional Baul-Kirtan Bhairavi but the words are about the colour red: '*Laal jey maa'yer shindur, laal ke keno bhoy...*' Red is the mother's shindur, why be afraid of red? None of the attentive middle-lower-middle-class audience looks like they've ever had to be afraid of the colour red or the *tara-haturi-kaastey* – the star, hammer and sickle – on the flags that flutter around the small ground.

The audience, the grandmothers, the babies, the state Special Security Unit safari-suits, the marriage lights among the swaying palm trees, the lone, perverse Trinamool flag on someone's gate, everything and everyone at Garfa-Katapukur is waiting for Senior Comrade Buddhadeb Bhattacharya, chief minister of West Bengal, to arrive on the penultimate night of his campaign to retain the Jadavpur seat he has held for twenty-nine years. The underdog anger, the fiery mountain of indignation, is now calmly hard-wired into righteousness in this core of the core constituency that's electorally buoyed the Left's rule over thirty years. Under their MLA, Comrade B, once young turk, now ageing lead tusker, this neighbourhood has moved from the quicksand of unauthorized refugee colony to the solid ground of *moddhobitto* demi-suburb and the people are here to show their *shroddha*, their faith, in the revolution that hasn't passed them by.

The singing ends and the warm-up speakers begin. 'If increasing food production by so many million metric tonnes is *awnyaay*, we want to be re-elected to continue that wrongdoing!' 'We will have to shed blood!' says another, as if he were speaking at a secret cell meeting in 1975, as if there hadn't been enough of an increase in the metric tonnage of bloodshed in the last ten years. The last speaker gives us this breakdown of recent history: 'For thirty years we brought peace and prosperity to this state. But for the last four-five years a negative force of anarchy has begun to spread unrest and violence. We have been losing ground to the terror of the Maoist Trinamool!'

As the speaker starts to delineate the struggle, the chief minister arrives in his Ambassador. As he walks up to the podium escorted by the SSU, ululations of Lalselaam-lalselaam-lalselaam break out at the edges of the gathering. Everyone applauds as he stands up to speak. For a moment the old gent searches for his teeth, but when his voice comes out, it is clear and sonorous. 'Comrades ... *bondhugon* ... *ma-bonera.*' There are no exclamations in his voice; there are hardly any of the dramatic rise and fall theatrics so loved by other Bengali political speakers. He is calm. Firm. Matter of fact. Simply telling the truth. Sad but confident. Apologetic. But quietly optimistic.

Suddenly my mind goes back to another election meeting in 1986: the afternoon maidan overflowing, it seemed, with all of Bengal. I was licensed by a video camera to stand close to the podium so I had a clear view of the two short dhuti-panjabied old men walking towards each other in joyous greeting. Jatin 'Jackie' Chakravarty was the slower of the two, Jyoti Basu lighter on his feet. As the two stumbled forward on the bumpy maidan turf, their arms jerked up in fists as if responding to a switch. 'Comrade!',

'Comrade!' 'Comrade, comrade!', 'Comrade!'. The two men hugged each other with their free arms, the two upraised Revolutionary fists unwilling to let go of the Revolutionary arms which were held up by the Revolutionary shoulder joints. I remember thinking these two couldn't have much time left, little knowing that they and their ghosts would still be with us twenty-four years later.

At one point, I managed to get on stage when JB was speaking, to get a shot of the masses stretching away over his shoulder. I remember thinking that this speech-making was hardly the stuff of legend, but there again I was wrong. No one now on the Left, and certainly not Com. BB, ever attempts to copy the great Jyoti-Basu-non-linear style of speaking: a growl, an anecdote, a dialogue he had with Indira, or with Rajiv (but they didn't listen!), an image, a sound, all of it a moving verbal collage but somehow forming a whole, convincing picture that relieved you of your precious vote. Then there are people who remember going a long way to hear the oratory of Shyamal Chakravarty and the very different way in which he put together his *'chhoto-chhoto kothaa'*, his tiny clusters of sentences, to create mass hypnosis. There are others who remember the brilliance of Ashok Mitra, 'a typical Bangal intellectual' who would draw out his sentences, somewhat in the manner of Sombhu Mitra, but whose wordplay, the mixing of classical *saadhu-bhasha* with gritty, daily vernacular pulled you into his sharp argument and super-erudite world-view.

I hear Buddhadeb Bhattacharya say the word 'hoshiari', cunning, and I think he's suddenly speaking in Hindi. Whose cunning, I wonder, till I realize he's speaking of the damage Pranab Mukherjee (who didn't listen to him) is causing the ready-made and hosiery industry in the state. As I listen, the Comrade comes back into an attack on the reactionary phalanx ranged against his party and government. 'Our struggle is not only against these forces but also against the media that is supporting them and the money behind that media.' I feel Com. B is looking straight at me, but as he continues I see it's just a trick of the light. The Comrade is actually looking up and addressing all the enemy satellites lurking in the night sky.

As I keep listening, I realize I'm listening to the self-obituary of an era. This is not the martyr's voice that anticipates a great, losing but noble struggle in the 1950s, this is not the excited hike of tone informed by the sense of the proximity of power in the late 1960s, this is not the trumpet of triumphant victory in 1977, full of stern intentions and a huge, huge stamina, this is not the holding chant of the 1980s or the angry, arrogant rant of the 1990s, this is the ledger of post-election excuses being read out by the chief book-keeper of Leftist grievance. Trinamool, the Maoists, the media, the Americans, the Hindu Right, the industrialists, the people who opposed friendly industrialists, the *sushil shomaaj* – civil society – anyone, everyone and their brother-in-law except the party and the Front themselves. Whichever way you look at it, I realize this is Comrade B's last stand in the electoral arena: even if by some miracle he trips back into his office in Writers' Building, he will not see out another term as leader.

I feel an odd warmth towards this man as I watch him, and I'm not sure where this comes from. It feels intrusive and wrong, this sympathy, but I can't help it. I feel bad for the decent man in him, the learned man, the film-buff, the avid reader, the poet and the playwright of whatever calibre he may be, but I can't bring myself to feel too bad for the mask of *shobbhota*, of civility, he has provided to the many who don't give a toss about culture or decency or humanity. I'd heard the Comrade had recently been reading Jose Saramago's novel *Blindness* and I can't but think that he surely must get the parallels between a whole society going blind and the one he has helped blind for so many years.

R-Day minus 16

Day Zero

On the sultry morning of polling in Kolkata, I'm invited to the Star Ananda TV panel. There is a festive air in the TV studio, everyone full of cakes and jokes as the large screen in front of us fills with a grid from different polling stations. As Left and Tinno personalities exchange barbs and arguments, studio boys crawl around under the cameras like soldiers in trenches, holding level plates of patties and pastries. Every now and then the anchor turns to one of us and asks a question and I can see some of my co-panelists trying to make sure they don't have a mouthful of Kathleen's Catering when their turn comes. After an hour of this, I wait for the cameras to pan away from my end of the table and sneak off for a cigarette break. I'm joined on the stairway by another journalist who is only slightly pro-Baamphont.

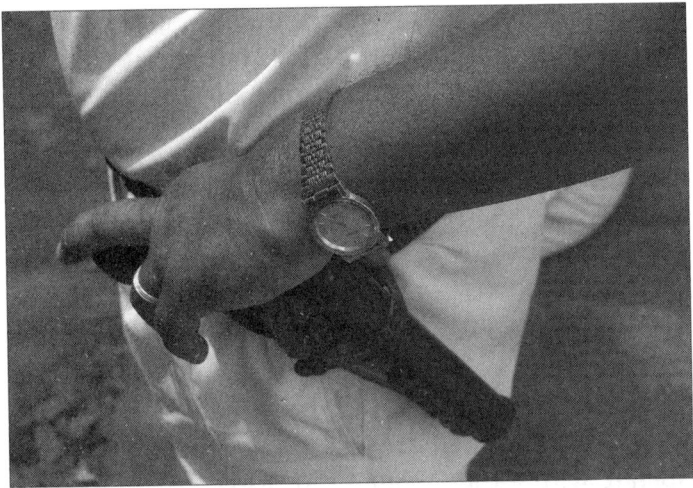

'Arre, you don't know what happened last year, do you? These people ran a programme that was somewhat critical of the railways and guess what? Within two days a couple of Railway Protection Force people landed up here to make threats. Can you believe it? RPF, which has no jurisdiction here! Imagine, if Mamata could do that as railway minister, what she will do once she's in power at Writers'?'

'Are you saying she's coming for sure?'

The journo gives his cigarette a hard time before answering. '*Ei, daikho ki hoy* but I think *aashchhey*. I would say majority of about thirty seats, for the *jote*, I mean, Trinamool-Congress *miley* together.'

By that afternoon, the hot sun is gone. It's almost as if even the weather realizes this is polling day in Kolkata. From the steamy morning the sky changes to an unseasonal grey by early afternoon, threatening rain. Moving around the city, I remember a few encounters with different people since the elections were declared.

Early in April, there are the two policement at a rally. For a mama, the man has a genial face with humour around the eyes. The eastern UP accent is crinkled too, after nearly fifty years of usage. 'You've been to villages, haven't you? So you've seen the cows, with the ropes around their necks? A cow strays into someone else's field and the farmer yanks it back with the rope, yes? Well, we policemen are like those cows. We always operate with a rope around our necks.'

'For instance, say we arrest a troublemaker during these elections.' The other black-white cop is Bengali, a bit younger and of a higher rank. 'Say we bring him to the thana. Who do you think gets into trouble?' The bhaiya mama translates. 'The bastard's party boss calls our OC and *we* get the *daant*, the ticking-off. *Tumi arrest koreccho, ekhon tumi bojho!* You've arrested him, so now it's your problem! So, we let him go. And you, the public, say we don't do anything.'

'When did you join the force?' I ask the UP man.

'One year after the Bum-Phrunt came to power, late 1978.'

'Are you planning to vote?'

The other man answers, 'No, dada, we don't vote. We stay in our police lines and we work crazy hours during these election periods. We just want it to be over quickly and with as little *jhaamela* as possible.'

'You've been in service for thirty-three years, wouldn't you like to serve under another administration?'

The Bong grins. 'Dada, we are what is called a disciplined force. We may feel like what you're suggesting, but we can't say anything!'

The cop from UP shakes his head. 'I have a registration in my home village, or I can also show my card here, but where do I get the time to go vote?' He looks at me with some sadness and points to the leather harness of his uniform. '*Yeh lohey ka pinjara jab tak rahega, hum kuchh bol nahin payengey.*' Till we're in this iron cage, our lips are sealed.

Today, I am trying to vote in a college building near my flat. Everything is clean and calm. The black-white cops seem happy to be playing third fiddle to the CRPF and the assorted armed uniforms loitering about the city. For all the fancy personnel and paraphernalia, the actual machine is hidden behind a simple half-box of brown cardboard. Every now and then a long electronic wail ensues from behind the cardboard and yet another voter comes out looking as if they do this every other day. A soldier of that other disciplined force, the Election Team, is complaining bitterly that there is as yet no sign of lunch. '*Bhaabtey paaro? Dokkhin Kolkataye election officers-der jonney kono khabar nei!*' Can you imagine there's no food arrangement for election officials in south Kolkata? I give it half an hour before the Rajasthani or Tamilian CRPF will need to deploy: keeping a middle-aged Bong babu away from his food is the first step on a very short route to Tahrir or Tienanmen.

Outside, the grey afternoon develops a fine spritz of rain. It already feels like early monsoon. Driving around south Kolkata, I feel like I'm in some special vehicle on a bandh day – the streets are empty, far emptier than on a normal Sunday, and silent. It's almost as if the city has run its batteries down, recharged them and is now rebooting. Devoid of even the normal off-day clutter, the streets and buildings intensify their personalities, some extremely beautiful, some surreal, with even the ugly concrete grunge looking like it could be easily dismantled. The streets take on the sparseness of a blank document screen on which some new drama is about to be typed.

On this polling day, we start from Minto Park and drive to Behala chowrasta; from there we make our way through New Alipur, past MamBan's house in Kalighat, through Rashbehari down to Jadavpur; taking Sukanta Setu, we get on to the winding road that comes out on the Eastern Bypass and chug up to the ITC hotel, and from there, through Park Circus, back to Minto Park. It's a pretty comprehensive *pradakshina* of south Cal and it would normally take over six hours; today it takes just under two hours, mainly because we are driving slowly, looking at the city. It's the kind of time I imagine Amit Mitra or some Delhi corporate cowboy would want to make every working day.

'It's not going to happen. There will be problem.' The voice of the Environmental Activist based in Delhi is laced with weary sarcasm. One of many Bengali boys who escaped Kolkata in the 1980s to make good in the Big Bad Bairey, his analysis is steady and precise as a fish-cutting *boti*: 'Amit-mittir is using this World Bank language of stakeholders in the state, like shareholders in a company. Problem *ta hochhey*, general people are not stakeholders, they are just people who need things. Like food, and justice, and good environment. *Ei profit-loss'er onko tey ora keno dhukbey?*' Why should they enter into this matrix of profit and loss?

'CPM tried to treat party faithful like favoured shareholders and now they are suffering because of that. These Mamata people will also suffer and also make us suffer with this trying, or rather pretending, to turn the state into a company in which people are forced to invest. People in this state know company from East India time! *Trinomool ke eitaar dividend khub kharap bhaabey kaamdabey.*' The dividend of this will bite the Trinamool very sharply.

At Behala, we turn around and re-enter the city limits. As a black-white mama checks our car papers, a hard-eyed commando tries to stare me down from under his black bandana, finger on the trigger of his AK. Earlier, we had driven past a posse of seven men walking silently at the side of the road. They were led by a tall man with muscles rippling out of the rolled-up sleeves of his dark-brown shirt. It was not clear which party he belonged to, but he too had a pretty good stare when I looked at him a beat too long.

Suddenly, a kind of near future becomes very clear to me – it doesn't take great clairvoyance. Whichever party the brown-shirted muscleman belonged to, people like him will wait. Even as whichever newly sworn-in finance minister of West Bengal tries to make the state safe for investocracy, these people will be out on the streets. The black-topped commando also has a rope around his neck. Once he's yanked back to his farm, the muscleman will come into play and the mama from UP and his colleagues will, I suspect, be quite busy.

R-Day minus 13

Indications of a Tiumph

'Boss, I love that coinage where you call them "Tinnomool" instead of 'Trinamool'. You can get away with it. If we wrote that, we'd get beaten up at Harish Chatterjee Street!'

A couple of days after the voting in the city, I'm at a dinner party on a roof terrace in south Kolkata. The crowd is a mix of journalists, academics and a few political people, all connected to the Left. PD, the man talking to me, is a veteran reporter who has to keep his nose clean with the Trinamool HQ at Harish Chatterjee Street in Kalighat. Another friend overhears and comes over.

'What do you mean, "coinage"? He didn't coin that, he just phonetically reproduced! That is what they do say, no? Tinnomul! In fact, all *raw-phola* and *ree-phola* words will officially be abandoned, in Bangla and English both!'

'I just repoduced,' I agree.

'Tiangular Purk,' says PD.

'It is a tavesty,' says the third guy.

'The Baamphont will have to made a tiage of their Politburo.'

'Politbudo.' Budo, meaning old man or geriatric.

We turn to another friend who's in the CPM's middle-hierarchy. 'Ei, Biplab! Ei Comr—comade! How will you taverse the long stetch in the opposition, haan? *Ektu bol to?*' Just tell us?

'Who told you we are going to be in the opposition? Have you seen how many voters have turned out in 24 Parganas?' Biplab, whose real name isn't Biplab, smiles confidently as he changes the CD. 'You people are going to look pretty foolish on the thirteenth, especially Ruchir and you lot who pay court at Harish Chatterjee Street.'

'Hey,' I protest, shouting over Credence Clearwater Revival screaming 'Born on the Bayou'. 'I haven't made any predictions, okay? In print or out. I've just said it would be great if you guys were finally out of power.'

'Yes, but you're writing for the main propaganda organ of the Trina – sorry, Tinnomul.'

'Have you read what I've been writing?'

Yes, Biplab has been reading my diary pieces, and yes, he agrees I haven't been the greatest cheerleader for MamBan or her party. Another CPM intellectual is standing next to the booze, arguing with PD about the projected numbers. Again the same conviction: the high voter turnout everywhere means the old loyal communist vote is coming out after many elections because they realize they need to save the situation; it will be close, but We Shall Overcome. After a while PD walks way from CPM 2 and shakes his head.

'*Ki?*'

'He's just not getting it. They are going to – they are already *getting* – thrammed. Badly.'

'You sure?'

'Yeah. They've still got some hope in Cooch Behar and in the Dinajpurs but as you come south, it gets worse and worse. Except maybe a couple of seats in 24 Parganas – maybe Rezzak Molla will survive there but otherwise it's over.'

'Bankura, Birbhum, Bardhaman?' I name the three districts that make up the Red Fortress.

'Game over, boss. I'm telling you.'

'Really?'

'Really. Except the CPM's got huge arms stockpiled in Bankura and Birbhum so there might be serious jhaamela after the results. Many Netais,' he finishes, referring to the massacre in January, where a group of cornered CPM cadre opened fire on a protesting mob.

Later, as the party winds down, Biplab grips my arm and pulls me aside. His earlier confidence is now drowned in Old Monk.

'You know what they will do if they win, don't you?'

'Who? Mamata-*ra*?'

'Who else? They will start picking off our people, Ruchir. One by one, they will kill our workers, especially us party members. You will get a knife here, one bullet there, a motorcycle accident at night, a hit and run…'

'They think you won't retaliate?'

Biplab doesn't hear my question. He grips my arm harder.

'They will come for us, Ruchir. Will you remember us, then? If something happens to me, you'll remember me, *na*? Nothing else, just remember me, okay? Write about it if you can, okay?'

R-Day minus 10

Day of the Vocusts

'Oh, I used to be a champion at stuffing vocus!' says Fatima, whose real name is not Fatima, cheerfully. 'I used to organize hundreds of vocus across three to four wards for the CPM.

'Vocus' is a truly beautiful word forged in the molten-metal factory of Howrah politics: an alloy of 'vote' and 'bogus', with a glaze of the 'focus' it must take to steal votes from non-voting citizens. Fatima, however, is now less than proud of her past achievements.

'One day, the local MLA came to visit and Z-bhai brought me forward and praised me to the skies, saying, "Fatima has done the maximum number of vocus voting for us!" The MLA patted my back. The moment they praised me, I began to sense I'd done something really wrong and shameful.'

If that was a first realization, another one followed soon afterwards. 'A local leader, G-bhai, asked me one night if I wanted to see Bangladesh. He said he could show it to me from the roof of this building. I wondered, "Bangladesh? From here? How?", but I went up with him anyway. The second Hooghly bridge was bright with lights. Eden Gardens *bhi chamak rahaa thha.*' Eden Gardens was also shining. Fatima pauses. 'But the basti below the building was dark. G-bhai pointed to the lights and said, "That's India." Then he pointed to the dark basti, grinned and said, "And that's Bangladesh." Then he started talking about various plans, connector roads, apartment blocks, shopping malls, all to be built once the basti was removed. I don't think he realized I actually live in that basti. There he was, calling *my* basti "Bangladesh". That woke me up.'

Bangladesh. Pakistan. What the novelist Sankar once called *Kolkata'r khata-paikhana*, Calcutta's service latrine. The workshop of Calcutta. Its manufacturing liver. The 'suburb' on the 'wrong' side of the river. The cockfighting pit. Today, on a properly hot May morning, Howrah, town and district both brace for the onslaught of all the different parties that want its vote, genuine or vocus. This is the mini 'Red Fort' the Trinamool wants to wipe out; this is where the CPM wants its Stalingrad, a redoubt to be held at all costs, from where the tide will turn; this is where the BJP has put in a lot of weight, as has the Janata Dal (Secular) and otherwise. In the rising summer heat, the streets and lanes of Howrah look not so much like a latrine as an explosion of lunatic urbanity: ugly, new, hyper-

coloured multistorey buildings rise out of a mess of grey-brown bastis and rusting old factory buildings; the shops that are open seem measly and ill-supplied, belonging more to a run-down mofussil town than the biggest urban adjunct of Calcutta; cycle-rikshas yaw wildly, the riksha-wallas unused to having so much space in the lanes that are usually stuffed with smoking traffic; people mill about on the corners, waiting to vote, waiting for trouble.

I say goodbye to Fatima, who refuses to tell me whom she's voted for. It's clear that she's ambiguous but equally plain that her loyalty to the Left Front is long gone. I join up with B, a young journalist who writes for a Calcutta Urdu paper, K, her colleague and photographer and my friend VR. The idea is to drive to three or four of the most troublesome booths and see if anything is happening. I ask if one can get a cup of tea somewhere. B laughs out loud. 'Not without a coupon today, it won't be easy!' she chortles. 'Coupon?' I ask. 'Yes, you need a coupon, from one or the other party. Then you can get tea, or even biryani. Without that, it's difficult on voting day.' B's colleague K adds this classic nugget: 'The candidate of X party spent so much money buying liquor and chicken for people, telling them to eat and drink and vote for him. But he made the mistake of stopping two days ago, so now the folks have gone over to where the other parties are serving food.' VR pipes up: 'The tiranga should be replaced with a flag with two motifs: a bottle and a chicken. That's what this country has become, all over, in every state!'

'Voters being given liquor is normal everywhere in India,' says B, acerbic now, 'but what do you say to the Bihari paramilitary brothers in uniform who got drunk the other day and began to molest us women? Do we say, bhai, let us be, we are also Bihari? Do we say go find some Bengali women to hassle? Even if we tried something nasty like that, do you think they'd listen? We had to make many calls and complain before someone pulled them back! You won't find that in the newspaper tomorrow. No one's going to write about that, it's all, look how wonderful the paramilitary are for giving us fair elections.'

As we move from booth to booth in urban Howrah, Bally and Liluah, there is an undertow of tension that was missing in most of the Calcutta polling. 'There's never been an election in Howrah without some serious trouble,' B tells me authoritatively. 'Every polling day, you'll get murders, bomb-maari, at least a hundred people arrested. This morning seems to be passing calmly, but it can't last. Just wait till afternoon.' Talking to people, the broader picture I get is this: if a fair vote happens, including a high-ish polling percentage, the CPM is in danger of being wiped out here; they can only counter by making it difficult for the Biharis and Marwaris to vote, and so the trouble is likely to brew up from those pockets; surprisingly, there's been nothing in the morning, except one shooting in Baksara which the local SP claims is not a political case, but people expect trouble from noon onwards.

In front of a major booth in a school, the Janata Dal (Secular) candidate smiles an oily smile at B. *'Aap pehle to yeh bataaiye ki aap didi hain ki behen hain? Uss sey rishtey mei fark hota hai*!' First tell me, are you an older sister or a kid sister, it changes the relationship. B is unimpressed by this unctuousness from the older man, she's seen too much of it from different party honchos, often followed by bullying and borderline violence when she's written something they don't like. 'Do you expect trouble here?' she asks Shri J-D (Secular). 'Well, these people are making a difference for sure,' he says, pointing to the CISF jawans checking IDs at the school gate. 'But who knows? Let's see what happens in the afternoon.'

At another school, in the Bally area, I ask a young paramilitary man if there's been any jhaamela. He looks at me with the contempt oversized Australian cricketers once used to reserve for Saurav Ganguly. *'Merey hote hue yahaan kiski himmat hai jhaamela karega?'* Who's going to have the guts to make trouble when I'm standing here? The guy is tall and fit, he has his sub-machine gun strapped across his back, and in his hand he carries a big *dandaa*. The trash talk is very effective – I certainly don't want to try and meddle with his booth.

Traditional booth-capturing now being a thing of the past, people try other techniques. Till mid-day the only problem seems to have been one presiding officer taking too long to process voters through, something seen as a CPM time-wasting ploy to reduce the opposition's score. *'Han, udhar slow-motion mey voting ho rahaa thha to usko hataa diya. Ab vahaan thiik hai.'* Yes, voting was in slow motion over there, so they removed him. Now things are fine. The person speaking is a sidekick to the local Congress boss. Walking away from the crowd around the booth, he's very clear that peaceful voting in Howrah means only one thing: *parivartan*. But he's also clear that this is temporary, that what Adhir Chowdhury has done in Mushidabad is the right thing. *'Abhi to hum unkey saath hai, baaki baad mey dekhiye kya hota hai.'* Right now we're with them (the TMC) but see what happens in the future.

Driving back from Liluah, a strange landscape unfurls, one ruled by its own slow-motion, empty rail tracks criss-crossing, green climbing up abandoned

factory chimneys, ponds and trees alternating with packed human habitation. All around us there is an overwhelming sense of great snail's-pace struggle yielding very meagre rewards. Nearing Howrah Station, we turn a corner and the driver suddenly brakes. In the middle of the crossing is a wheelchair with a very old woman curled inside it. Journalists are crouching around her, asking questions and firing their cameras. K, the photographer, gets out to join them, and so do I. We all take photographs of Uma Rani Ghosh, ninety-five years of age, being taken to cast her non-vocus vote.

When I've come here previously VR has pointed out to me that here in Shibpur, Howrah, is one terminus of the legendary Grand Trunk Road with the other one being in Peshawar. 'At that end you have Osama bin Laden and at this end you have someone like B, who has a very different notion of Islam,' VR is fond of saying. On the day after one end of GT Road is finally freed from Osama bin Laden, I watch this surreal sight at the other end of the old highway in the company of this feisty young woman who has very different conceptions not only of Islam, but also of democracy and communism, not to mention all the old men trying to retain control over these belief-systems.

4

R-Day minus 9

Highway West

The white cloud is a huge zeppelin slash against the black evening sky. We are on NH 6, the highway that leads west out of Calcutta towards Chennai and Bombay. The road north may still look the same as a decade ago but the small towns lining this road are built-up, with all kinds of shops, dhabas and factories. Except for the Bangla signage and the classic eastern Indian landscape of paddy fields and banana groves, except for the huge kaalboishaakhi brewing, the broad and new tarmac could have been in Haryana or Punjab.

We stop for tea near a roundabout where large articulated trucks slash by. There is an official Gypsy parked outside the 'hotel' which to all purposes looks like a motel. Sitting inside, staring balefully at the IPL game on TV are three CRPF officers of reasonable rank. It's not clear whether they are heading into the business end of the polling or away from it after an inspection.

We enter Medinipur town through small, dark, back streets spattered with rain. This is the centre for the last two phases of the election, the two trickiest areas in terms of security: Purulia district and Lalgarh area in West Medinipur, with their recent history of Maoist upheaval and CPM Harmad retaliation. In our hotel, The Hindustan, rooms are in short supply, huge swarms of politicians and media people having descended on this, the final arena.

I meet up with a journalist who's been trawling through the whole tribal zone which is called Jongol Mohol, Junglemahal. He's someone who has been here for the last few elections and I ask him if he expects trouble.

'Things do seem quiet but can't really say. In any case the paramilitary and cops' bandobast is huge. Apparently they are even bringing in mine-clearing vehicles.'

5

R-Day minus 8

The Shop on the Right Is Still on the Right

Barely twenty kilometres out of Medinipur, you enter a zone of myth.

There's a hump bridge over a nala, with low, white-painted stones on each side – *this is where the chief minister's convoy was attacked with a landmine, which set off police reprisals, which set off the* andolon, *the whole movement.*

You pass a small, bored police checkpost – *the action began from here, two years ago this was the start of the no-go area, after this,* kaataa-rasta, *roadblocks, Maoists checking which media group you were from. Things could get very nasty because the police had used a van with a national TV channel's logo to go in.*

Open fields growing nothing very much, dotted with clumps of forest, and then a CRPF post: razor-

wire dancing around tin-roof huts, a dirty concrete toblerone slab of latrines, sandbag squares – *this is exactly where we crawled under fire, one of the Haryanvi CRPF troop commanders cursing cowardly, sister-fucking Bungali police as he diffused a chain of landmines with his teeth, as he handed his boys the tin cans saying,* 'Ley betey, tera tiffin khaa ley!' *Here, son, here's your tiffin-box, eat.*

Villages pass, the saddest sight for anyone with any nostalgic pull towards Tagore's Bengal or even that of Gopal Ghosh or Jamini Roy: the typical, conical thatched roofs of the village huts now reproduced in drooping tin, the corrugated metal toasting under the May morning sun. Every now and then, a solar panel stitched on the roof, whether tin or traditional *khawr*. On the verticals of the tiny, naked shops and rusty booths, a shifting medley of flags: the Baamphont's star, hammer and sickle, the Tinno's two-leaf clover, the Sheepeeaai's red-yellow sickle and sheaf of wheat, the JMM's green standard with Shibu Soren's face paired with a bow and arrow, the visibly fattening lotus of the BJP, the ragged green and white stripes of the Jono Shadharoner Shomity, or the People's Committee against Police Atrocities (PCPA).

The Jhitka Jungle begins in earnest, with stands of sal and *shegun* trees tripping away into the horizonless distance – *this is where it got really dangerous, but the Haryanvi CRPF man navigated us through with his map and compass.* After a while, we decide to stop. My guide pauses his story and the noise of bullets ceases. With the car engine off, the silence in the forest is total. After a few moments you realize it is not silence at all but a different kind of soundscape: bird calls from the *ghughu pakhi* and *kokil*, crickets amassing their buzz, the flap of odd wings, and, amidst all this, a busy, highway of red ants crawling inaudibly up the trunk of a tree, one cluster freighting a large dead insect. We savour this for a while and carry on.

Entering Lalgarh, there's another blast site, just a few yards from the police station, and a college of 'English Learning' named after Amartya Sen. A bedraggled townlet, the pakka road ending where the muddy marketplace begins. A small brawl of buses crowned with people, luggage and tied chickens on the roofs and then we are through, out on to the other side. On the small country road heading towards Bhim Chowk and Boro Peliya we suddenly see fifteen or so schoolgirls on bicycles, a mobile flock of colour that makes you wonder if you've strayed into some Nitishian elysium in Bihar. A little later we stop at a few roadside huts next to a large, opaque pond.

My guide hasn't been here since 2009 but he recognizes the place. 'One advantage to the government ignoring Junglemahal is that I could find this easily. Nothing's changed! The shop on the right side of the road is still on the right!' We see a man and my guide calls out. '*Eijey*, Shyamal?'

The man turns to nod and my guide says, '*Mota hoye gechhish!*' You've got fat.

I look at the thin man in pant-shirt and wonder how much thinner he could have been.

The village is on the other side of the road but we head to the small clutter of tea shop, cycle-repair shop and nondescript huts. About ten men are sitting around, clearly waiting for something. Their motorcycles are parked along an earth road that leads into the fields, each bike bearing the green and white *potaka* of the PCPA. None of them seem to be armed.

The chat throws up small conjectures: Mamata may be coming to Jhargram tomorrow. Their own leader, Chhatradhar Mahato, may be temporarily released from jail to address a political meeting before electioneering closes in three days. The dreaded CPM Harmad boss, Anuj Pandey, has been seen in the area; he's obviously come back to threaten people before the campaign, but

he could be arrested. My guide looks at a large, newly cleaned *haandi* and asks what's been cooking. It seems that the men had a good meal of meat and rice last night, to fuel them up for today's village campaigning. 'Rice and meat,' says my guide quietly, 'but meat doesn't mean mutton.' I raise my eyebows. 'Dog meat,' he explains. 'Mutton is too expensive here.'

I ask Shyamal to explain what the PCPA wants. He turns to me and speaks intensely, a film of sweat lining his eyes. *'Shudhu Maa-Maati-Maanush bolley to cholbey na?'* You can't just keep going on about 'Mother, Land and People'. You don't see the adivasis as mothers or sisters or people. *'Shara desher loker oporey tumi* bulldozer *chaaliye jachchho aar eikhaane tumi tai kortey chaao.'* You're rolling bulldozers over people across the country and that's exactly what you want to do here as well. *'Cholbey na.'*

'Next, crucial thing, lift the military. They are everywhere, people can't go into the jungle because the paramilitary are sitting there, guns pointing, staring at you. Mamata says she will declare this a disturbed zone, does she think that will actually help? Then, development. There's nothing here. If someone doesn't collect wood or leaves one day their pot won't have a fire under it the next day.'

As Shyamal starts to speak about the health situation, other men crowd around us. 'If someone so much as gets diarrhoea here, the doctor throws up his hands. He straight says, "Referred to Medinipur"! If a pregnant woman has any problem – Medinipur *rifaar!*' A small chorus begins, minor ailments and life-threatening illnesses listed and punctuated by 'Rifaar!' 'Rifaar!' 'Rifaar!' with one single contradictory bell-chink of '*Shudhu slaaine thhakey, aar kichhu nei!*' They can only give saline drips, nothing else.

Shyamal puts an end to the chorus. '*Ora shob bhote keliye niye jaay, phirey keu takaay o na!*' They all grab the votes and go, none of them even turns back to look.

After a while, we hear a motorbike. Their leader Manoj Mahato, Chhatradhar Mahato's point man in the world outside jail, arrives, riding pillion. MM is in his late twenties, far more dapper than his troops, neat shirt tucked into dirt-sweeping flares, a trendy, slim pair of clouded specs perched below a haircut that makes him look like a very sleek hedgehog. MM clearly has the same relationship to smiling as one of his political adversaries, Mamata Banerjee – it's not

a hobby in which he indulges. After some talk, the men get on their bikes and ride off in a convoy. MM drives with us to his party office in Bhim Chowk – it looks very much like another tea shop – and settles down to talk.

Answering my questions, MM goes over the same ground Shyamal has just covered, except he feels he has to do it in declamatory speech mode. I find myself switching off from what he is saying and watching the man instead. Behind the clouded spectacles, MM's eyes are far away as he speaks of the lack of development and health. He insists his party has always followed a legal, non-violent andolon, often besmirched by opponents and Maoists wanting to glom on to the movement. He demands to know why MamBan has betrayed them by declaring that Chhatradhar has taken money from the CPM to stand for these elections. He states that all sorts of political parties may say they back the PCPA but the Committee will chart their own course for the uplift of tribals regardless of pretend or real *samarthan*. Listening to Shyamal, I could see the poverty the PCPA is talking about. Looking at Manoj Mahato, I see the poverty of the man, the young 'leader' who's been thrust into this role, this man who doesn't meet my eyes, who reaches for the formula whenever he can.

Every now and then, as he talks, Manoj receives phone calls; his mobile releases one of those sub-Mangeshkar women's voices singing, '*Subah Sai, shaam Sai, Shirdi ke Daataa...*' After the fourth time, I ask him why he has a bhajan to the Sai Baba as a ringtone.

MM looks baffled. 'I believe in no God or religion,' he says. 'One of the boys put this on my phone and I paid no attention to it.'

My guide joins in the ribbing. 'And why do you have a Bangla love song as your caller tune, then?' Again, MM shakes his head till we dial his number and play it for him on another phone.

Leaving Lalgarh, something Manoj Mahato says comes back: 'None of the parties are talking about us, they are all talking about bringing "investment" to Jongol Mohol. Now, if Jindal comes in and puts a wall around 38 sq. km of our land, and builds an ore-processing *karkhana*, how does that help us adivasis? They will take our iron ore and, once it's finished, they will up and go. We will still be left where we are.'

Why is this, I ask him. And why does he think the CPM has done literally nothing for this area in thirty-odd years?

One reason, the same reason. *'Ora amaderke maanush bhaabhei na.'* They don't think of us as humans.

The other thing of interest MM has mentioned is CPM Harmad boss Anuj Pandey's fancy house in Dharampur, a CPM enclave some distance away. 'Where did that house come from, in the middle of that poor village? With whose money was it built?' I know that a gang allegedly made up of Maoists and Trinamool cadre have destroyed the house and the Baam's party office close by. I don't ask MM if he was part of the mob that attacked the house and office. Having seen the shop on the wrong side of the road, I now want to see the condition of the shop on the left side.

As the sun heats towards noon, we head for Dharampur. As we bump over the ghosts of old roadblocks, I wonder if MM is making up the rumour or whether the dangerous Anuj Pandey is indeed back.

5

R-Day minus 8

The House the Left Built

Driving from Lalgarh to Jhargram, the topography is different from the Jhitka jungle, which we passed through this morning. The jungle is interrupted by cultivated fields, river beds and built-up areas. My guide again begins to point out sites: the Naxals could move freely on motorcycles across that low bridge you see over there. This is where the CRPF had a temporary camp. Passing through a village, car windows up, his voice still drops – *'Eikhaane Harmad shobdo ta jorey boltey nei,* CPM*'er elaaka.'* You don't say the word 'Harmad' too loudly around here, this is a CPM enclave.

I try and connect this zone to Bosnia and Croatia, to Rwanda or Sudan but the comparisons fail. There is an ethnic element to the conflict here, sure, between imported Bangals and local adivasis of different tribes,

between Bengalis and Biharis, but then there are also the tiers: the fight between local interests and wider agendas, between Lalgarh/Jhargram, Medinipur, Calcutta and Delhi. This is also the eastern edge of the network of Mao-Mao pockets that stretches all the way across the belly of India like a suppurating, irregular appendix scar. This is also the blood-soaked set of squares on one side of the larger Bengal chessboard, littered with knocked-over red and green pawns that Grandmasters Baam and Tinno have forgotten to remove.

We are now looking to examine one such square left behind by a still alive but absconding pawn. 'I think it's down this road,' says the guide, asking the driver to turn off the highway.

We bump past ramshackle half-pakka huts and the odd concrete building into the village of Dharampur. After more of the rusty tin pagodas, we come to a clearing. The CPM party office is a low, PWD-style construction, the open ground in front of it fenced by wire, with newly printed red flags flying from each post. The windows of the building look like they've been bombed out and then replaced by new grilles around which the concrete is still wet and deep brown. Three carpenters sit on the grass, sawing new doors. There are three party workers lounging in chairs under a tree. I look right and see why they are so relaxed. Abutting the party office grounds is a huge newish-looking CRPF compound, the concertina wire almost slicing into the simple wire of the party fence. 'All our leaders are out, we have no one who can talk to you.' We make small talk and then slip in that we wouldn't mind seeing Anuj Pandey's house, or whatever's left of it.

We walk down a wide mud road, the tin dunce caps of the huts reflecting heat. I'm not sure what I'm expecting but I walk right past the small, white, two-storey bungalow before the man stops me. '*Eita. Eita Anuj Pandey'r baadi.*' This is Anuj Pandey's house.

One of the few times Manoj Mahato, the second-in-command of the PCPA, had shown any passion was when he spoke of this house: with whose money did the dreaded Pandey build such a fancy house?

What I see is a typical, shoddily constructed bonsai-castle you find all over Bengal – the kind built by some petty nouveau-riche or a mid-level government officer with no taste and not too much of a bribery-pension. Bits of the house have been gutted and someone has clearly taken a hammer to some of the protruding bits. Looking at the bungalow and its sad conceit, I realize I've been searching for the wrong comparisons: this is not former Yugoslavia or Africa, this is more Garcia Marquez territory, the eternally long civil war as insidious and unending as tropical rain, the 'war' itself a kind of fraternal mayhem where everyone's known each other for generations.

Two houses down, a middle-aged man in a *genji* and lungi sits at a desk inside his small porch. 'Come and sit,' he says. 'I am Anuj's older brother.' Sitting among open newspapers under his wax sealing pots, Bimal Pandey looks like no one's written to him in a long

time. Like Manoj Mahato, he doesn't meet my eyes very much, but when he does, he projects a weirdly confident sadness. What will happen in the local elections? 'Oh, fifty-fifty in Jhargram.' But this is a Left stronghold, surely? 'Maybe, but which stronghold can we be sure of now? There are people daring to stand up to the party in Bardhaman, on the open road, in daylight. It's over.' His tone is flat but there is no hesitation. What will happen then? 'Oh, if the Front wins, they will go back to militancy. But if we lose, the youth who'd gone to the Maoists will return and join the Trinamool, which is good. Shubhendu Adhikari has brought some of them back into TMC already. So these boys will return and and stay with electoral politics and there will be peace.'

I sit, watching the newspaper flutter under the sealing pots. Pandey shakes his head apropos of nothing and answers a question I haven't asked. 'Those who think they can fight the CPM without guns are stupid.' He smooths down the newspaper and continues talking, lucidly, but almost to himself. 'It will become like '72 to '77 again. Did you ever read the *Ananda Bazar* and *Jugantar* of that time? You'll see there's hardly any mention of the CPM. It'll become like that again. The Congress goondas who infiltrated the party will leave.' A pause to smooth thinning hair. 'Is it a joke? People gathering in streets to protest against the CPM in Bardhaman? In Nirupam Sen's area? *Amar kaachh theke likhenin, Nirupam Sen o dawsh hajar votey haarchhey.*' Write it down from me – even Nirupam Sen's going to lose by ten thousand votes.'

Pandey first shakes his head at the thought of the top Baamphont leader going down and then acknowledges what he's saying with a nod, looking away all the time. '*Bhaalo. Herey geley CPM shuddho hobey.*' Good. If it loses, the CPM will become purified.

Driving back to Medinipur, we get confirmation of the mine-clearing vehicles rolling in near Kaata Pahar on the Jharkhand border. On the highway, we pass more CRPF bunkers, a road-opening party of paramilitary spreading along the highway, the litter of sandbags that marks another dismantled Harmad 'bunker' and, finally, another sad, small, ugly building at the side of the road, this one yellow. 'That used to be the Harmad's Enayatpur HQ,' says my guide. Once bristling with guns and handcrafted ordnance of all sorts, the place now looks ready to be snapped up by some small-town builder. The suddenly smooth road makes me drowsy and I almost dream of little red ants crawling across 1970s' Bangla newsprint, hanging on effortlessly as the wind makes the pages rise and fall under them. These are not the large, nutritious semi-transparent red ants the Naxals make into what I now think of as Mao Marmalade, but the nasty, tiny, red city ones that used to picnic on you as you sat on the grass.

6
MAY

One Week to R-day

The Factory on the Moon

The flowers are out on the trees in Medinipur town, yellow ones, red ones, and the passing loudspeakers seem to make them shake as various people belt out their last speeches. A convoy of white SUVs blasts by, carrying MamBan, followed by Sultan Singh's maroon Innova, all headed to a final meeting before electioneering ends this evening. There's a long queue at a *bhaja'r dokaan*. Past it, I hear someone say, 'TMC *aashbey*, 160-up *to hobei hobey*.' The TMC is coming, with more than 160 seats. Given that the strongest local liquor is called '60-up', this sounds more like a lethally high-proof brew than an election result.

The Rose Valley Hotel is where the Tinno have set up their camp and the staff at Reception look like they've already imbibed some of the new distillation of self-importance. Families and minor politicos crowd the

lobby as waiters push through, carrying orders. We walk to the booze shop behind the hotel but we are too late. All the shops shut forty-eight hours before polling, to reopen only well after the booths have closed, which in the case of Medinipur means another five whole days, since the town is included in both the last phases. I'm heading back towards happily wet Kolkata the next day, but the journalists who have to be here till the tenth are desperate, all except one smug TV man whose doctor has ordered him to stop drinking. *'Daikh, toder ekhon shisto paalon korte hobey,'* he says. *'Aar Didi eley, aaro shisto!'* Look, you all will have to follow discipline from now on. And once Didi comes, even more discipline.

Outside, a lonely van passes by, broadcasting the BJP's final message: 'We don't need Harmads or Maoists, we need progress! Make the BJP victorious by a big margin!' I suddenly have a vision of the Left Front sweeping back to power in five years' time, riding on some rejuvenation wave, and then 'managing' the 'new' Bengal. I see them striding proud, sleek, bullish and quite Trinomulish after ten years, with many people here having forgotten about communist brutality just as people seem to have forgotten about Modi's mass murders in Gujarat.

The next morning, however, I find myself in a village in south Medinipur's Pingla Thana where there is no defeat or recapturing power for the Baamphont. My old friend Dukkhoshyam Chitrakar is very clear: 'I don't know what they did elsewhere, but here the Left have done very well by us. *Aagey aamra jigish kortam "ki khaabo?", ekhon aamra jigish kori "ki diye khaabo?", aar amader bhaater shomoshya nei!'* Earlier, we used to ask 'what will we eat?', now we ask 'what will we eat it *with*?', we no longer have a problem about the basic rice. Dukkhoshyam reminds me of what this village used to look like when I'd last visited, not that I need reminding. In 1986, the scroll painters' village of Naya looked a lot like the villages I've just seen in Junglemahal, just a hundred-odd kilometres to the north-west.

We'd arrived at Naya late at night and the dim hurricane lights illuminating the small bare huts was something I'd never seen before. Neither had I forgotten the worry on the villagers' faces, roused from their night's sleep at 9 p.m., till they saw we had brought along sacks of rice and daal. The next morning threw a hard sun on the poverty but also the great, unrecognized wealth being produced in the village. From the stark interiors of the huts the painters of Naya brought out their *pats*, the traditional scroll-paintings that are among the earliest forms of audio-visual communication in South Asia. I had a clear memory of that explosion of colour against the bare, light brown earth of their *uthons*. The sound of their voices putting song to the pictures had also stayed with me.

That was only the ninth year of the CPM's rule in Bengal. Now, a quarter-century later, that spare village is gone, as is the long bumpy walk from the nearest motorable road. Naya is now right next to a pretty good tarmac road, electric connections are evident in all the houses, and the colourful wall paintings that decorate the entrances to the dwellings have to fight with rampant greenery. Walking through the tiny lanes, we are taken to the focus of the village, a modern, red-brick Painting Centre built with EU money and put together intelligently with the consultancy of various NGOs. As I approach, the kids come running, yelling '*Dotcom eshchhey, dotcom eshchhey*', imagining I'm from one of the organizations, the names of which end in '.com'. I look around the Centre and its unpretentious lines are quietly impressive: a large space for painting and workshops, guest rooms and bathrooms, lovely design for light, *patuas* sitting and working on a big project that has to be delivered two days after the election results are out.

Many things have changed, but thankfully not all. In the late 1960s, a cheeky young Dukkhoshyam had been put in jail for lampooning the great Congress duo of Atulya Ghosh and Prafulla Sen, when he sang: '*Haay Prafullo, Haay Atulyo, keu chhilo na toder tulyo, aaj kothaay gelo shei shob mulyo?*' Oh, Prafullo, oh, Atulyo/ the two of you were incomaparable, you know/ now tell me, where did your power go?

Today, sitting in the modern Centre, Gurupada Chitrakar sings us another song: *Apnara bhebe bolun shobai miley, ei kemon rajniti? Jano baara bhaatey chhai podilo, paanta bhhatey ghee, eita kemon rajniti?* All of you now think and say, what is this politics you see? Like ashes in freshly served rice, as if in stale rice fresh ghee, what is this politics you see? *Mone chhilo boro asha, amaar chhele aar hobey na chaasha, lekha-pora shudhu bhorosha, chaakri paay jodi, eita kemon rajniti?* Had great hope that my son wouldn't be a farmer like me, in schooling we trusted, so he could find work in a factory, what's this politics you see? *Jomi tey pholai sonar phoshol, laabh to doorer kotha, hoy na aashol, komey gechhey mone'r bol, ki hobey goti, eita kemon rajniti?* From the land we grow a golden harvest, forget profit – don't even make back the investment, our spirit's starting to seep, what is this politics you keep?

Gurupada says the song is about the shutting down of the Singur project but its slant is not that easy to decipher. Even in this village that's so grateful to the Left, the deep ambivalence, the scepticism of the immutable Bengal resistance gene rises in these artists.

They don't have any easy solutions, or very many songs you can turn into propaganda. Gurupada's song about Nandigram seems to start with a straightforward criticism of the Central police forces who come to establish peace: *Nandigramey shanti thhakbey, maanush thhakbey na*... peace will flourish in Nandigram, but no people will flourish there. But it moves quickly to the dilemma: 'We'll let you make a factory but we won't give up our land', and then to an anthem about how 'everyone knows we are are a farmer-centric land' before asking, '*taholey karkhana ki chaandey hobey, bhebe tomra bolo na*'. So will you make the factory on the moon, think and say all of you.

Before I leave, I visit Suvarna Chitrakar's house and she shows me her brilliant renderings of the movie *Titanic*, complete with a Kate Winslet nude, and of 9/11, with the face of Osama as the head of the aircraft going into a tower. Walking out of the village, I see food simmering in pots, raw mango pickle boiling, fish slices glistening, potato slivers frying. There seems to be plenty to eat with the basic rice and so, yes, there is support for the party that brought them all this, or that was ruling when the various crafts groups and NGOs managed to help the patuas pull themselves out of abject poverty. But looking at the scrolls depicting everything from Tagore's glories to Osama's crimes to Jyoti Basu's life, it hits me once again that the real 'tradition' the patuas of Naya uphold is one of criticism and satire. They have always been Bengal's audio-visual conscience keepers, its serious cartoonists. No matter who wins on Friday, no matter who takes the oath of

office, they will need to be aware that in the long run, he or she may just be material for a scroll painting made in Naya. Whether the scrolls are complimentary, worshipful or scathing will depend on the politics they keep.

11

R-Day minus 2

CIA Substation Calcutta

The Kolkata I return to is sizzling under the surface with a strange excitement. The city has voted and is pretending to get on with other things but everybody has an eye on the calendar. The violence people anticipated in February hasn't happened. There has been a startlingly high percentage of voter turnout. The EC and the paramilitary have done an exceptional job and the results will reflect what people really want. The hotels are filling up with foreign press-wallas arriving to catch the climax scene of this movie while extra OB vans from the big TV channels are driving across the country to be there on counting day. A journalist from the American National Public Radio comes over to do a short interview.

'The CPM people are saying the CIA is playing a huge role helping the Trinamool in these elections. Do you think this is true?'

I burst out laughing so my answer is unusable. We do a retake.

'I think the CPM has delusions of grandeur. If I was one of those Langley execs sent out to survey which Agency stations could be shut down, I think Calcutta would be on top of my cost-cutting list,' I finally manage.

Gautam Gambhir's KKR team, in the meanwhile, are fighting off any investors who might want to shut them down. In another match under loaded skies crackling with lightning, they manage to defeat Dhoni's assorted Madrasis, keeping alive their hopes for a berth in the IPL top group.

A couple of days before the results, I meet one of Kolkata's best political theorists at the Lake Club.

'I haven't been out of Calcutta myself this time, but from what I'm hearing there is no late Left surge.'

'I think it's over for them,' I agree.

'Yes, but Alimuddin Street doesn't know it. They are in some bubble.'

Like PS a month earlier in the Salt Lake bar, PT also thinks the real game is only just starting.

'You know, a whole different Bengal has come up under the communists' radar, come up despite them. You have small entrepreneurs doing little business here and there, you have a guy with a van who moves stuff from village to village, you have someone with a chain of three or four shops in a district, you have people running small manufacturing units. They are not rich but they are not working-class either, just above lower-middle class, I would say. All this has happened in the last twenty years and these are not people who fit into the Left's classic breakdown of farmer and worker and neither are they going to respond too long to *maa, maati, maanush,* if Mamata doesn't deliver. The next few years should be interesting.'

'How long does MB have for her honeymoon, do you think?'

'Oh, shorter than one would imagine. People will want to see serious change in eight or nine months, so I'd say next Jan-Feb at the outside. Otherwise you'll get widespread unrest.'

'Will she mess it up, do you think?'

'Maybe not. Depends on her majority. If it's a close result, I don't think she'll be able to handle the pressure. But if it's a large margin, she might muddle through to doing something. It won't be elegant, but then, after all these years, who cares about elegant except us intellectuals?'

'What about post-election violence?'

PT shakes his head. 'I know people are worried but I don't think too much will happen. At least, not right now.'

Redderdammerung

At ten past eight on the TV channel where I'm giving my tuppence of recently acquired insights, the scoreboard for West Bengal flicks up its first number: 'Others' = 1, which is a lead for the BJP. Tamilian wiseman Cho 'Cartoon' Ramaswamy is on the other link, wearing his white tilak and I realize I've forgotten to put on any war paint. Shortly, the other scoreboards start tripping and I'm reminded that Kolkata right now is the centre of the universe for only a few million people. I fight the temptation to mainline TV numbers and get out of the studio after my slot is over.

At Lake Market, it's like a normal morning. I notice the flower stalls have a large number of wreaths lined up, all made up from white flowers, and I wonder who will get them. In honour of the teeming millions of south India (Tamil Nadu, Pondicherry and Kerala) whose verdict will be heard today, I order some breakfast at

Prema Vilas. Waiting for my *idli-dosai*, I eavesdrop on two old gentlemen at the next table.

'CPM leading in the North, 10, and Trinamool in six here,' says one man.

'Yes, those TMC ones are around Kolkata,' replies the other man.

'The CPM's fight is still against America!' declares the first man and his friend nearly spits out his *vada*.

'America? How are you bringing in America today? Don't be silly!'

They are like characters from some version of *Waiting for Godot*. I note Samuel Beckett's spirit is still alive and well in my city and get into the car.

By the time I reach the crossing of Park Street and Lower Circular from Lake Market – in all of twenty

minutes – the game is sliding away very quickly. I'd
been planning to circle around Shyambajar before
returning to the CPM's HQ in Alimuddin Street, but
the information on the mobile instructs my good sense
otherwise. I get off at the mouth of Alimuddin Street
and start walking towards the CPM party office. The
last time I'd come here was the day after Jyoti Basu
died and the atmosphere was far more cheerful then.

Outside the building, the police are not even trying
to look busy. Inside the gates, everybody, the press
and party workers, all have the neutral expressions of
people who want no truck with joy or sorrow. 'What
is there?' their eyes seem to be saying. 'This happens.
Everybody has to go sooner or later.' As white Amby
after white Amby turns in from the lane, the press
crowd sizzles with manoeuvres; photographers take
out their tension by shouting at each other; party men
snap at the photographers to move back when they've
already moved back. The Ambys discharge nondescript
Stalin-worshippers, who all walk into the office with
their eyes dead straight. Not one journalist asks them
anything, not one photographer lifts a camera. We're
all waiting for Buddhababu to arrive. He's trailing by a
thousand votes by now and the Tinno-jote is leading in
160-odd overall in the state. It isn't even 10 a.m. yet.

When Buddhadeb Bhattacharya does arrive, the press
swirl around him, making him the centre of a small
typhoon. Within seconds he is inside the building,
climbing those famous stairs and then out of sight.
As we exit the gates, some cops who've been close

to him talk sadly about having given him their last salute. Further down the street towards the main road, the black-white uniform song is different and, oddly enough, echoes Manoj Mahato in Lalgarh: *'Bhaaloi hoyechhey gechhey, shuorer bachhara! Aamader ke kokhhono manusher moton dekhe ni!'* Good the sons of pigs have gone, they never saw us as humans.

A bit later, it's as if I've landed in another state altogether. From the midpoint of Harish Mukherjee Road, you can see the roadblocks and the little gatherings of people waving TMC flags. At a small *pandal*, people are shouting as the lead tally changes on a Bangla channel. A completely green man, covered in Trinamool's colour, thrusts a cup of tea in my hands and almost starts to cry. 'I'm thirty-eight, dada, and since I've had sense I've only known these people in power! Can you imagine what a day this is for me?'

I can imagine, but I don't need to. In the narrow lane in front of the Didi's house, there is a huge press of green-hued humans. Dancing, singing, waving men lifting grown, heavy women onto shoulders, other strong-looking women walking up and down, swaying, drunk without intoxicants, not knowing what to do with their elation. Green powder flies in the air, green powder carpets the street, green sweat trickles down cheeks. Bare-bodied men spin around, covered in skin paint, one nipple surrounded by an orange flower, the other by a green one. There is ten times as much press here than at Alimuddin, most of them teetering on a makeshift platorm in front of the TMC office. It gets

more and more difficult to move as you get closer to the office and, after a while, I give up. Except, to get out is also now near impossible. Bizarrely, over the mad cacophony of drums and shouting, the loudspeakers waft Rabindra Sangeet. Green sweat, orange sweat, white sweat, eyes glazed, a sea of smiling, grinning disbelief. I fight my way out of this *chakravyuha* of joy and get back to the car.

Half an hour later, crackling Rabindra Sangeet still accompanies us, but in a quiet lane in Santoshpur. *'Nai, nai bhoy, hobey, hobey joy, khule jaabey ei dwaar...'* No, there is no fear, there will, there will be victory, these doors will open.

Nirmal Ray and Lali Ray, two middle-aged Tinno workers, are pulling out huge hoardings that have been prepared days in advance: photo-shopped faces of Buddha, Biman and Gautam Deb in enlarged stills from the 1980s Bangla Bachchan-starrer *Anusandhan*. The line above them is less than Rabindric: *Phete gelo, pheshe gelo Kaliramer dhol*. Drum's burst, drum's worn out, Kaliram's drum. *'Eita ami mon-ey kori ekta mini-shaadhinota!'* says Lali. To me, this feels like a mini-Independence.

We are invited upstairs into someone's flat: old, red floors, neat, simple furnishings, and TV under a doily on which MamBan is addressing the nation in English. '...there will be the winning of the pippl!' she declares. Two minutes later, she switches to Bangla and instructs people to let new crowds through. *'Aapnara badi giye, chaan-taan korun!'* You all go home and get a bath.

Thinking about drums, I remember the completely worn-out drum I saw thirty-four days ago, at the rally of marginal groups in Subodh Mullick Square. No matter what happens to the CPM's drums, I wonder how that protesting man's drum will sound now.

15

R-Day plus 2

London

I have twisted my friend N's arm to accompany me to the airport. N hasn't taken kindly to the arm-twisting but he has been made to agree with promises of large shares of duty-free Single Malt upon my return. We both carry some wear and tear as we climb into the taxi early in the morning: MamBan may have stopped her supporters from celebrating too enthusiastically but no one was going to stop N, other friends and me from suitably marking the end of the Baamphont rule, which had begun in the year before I became an adult, when the now balding N was all of seven years old.

As the taxi makes its way through an empty Park Circus crossing we find ourselves laughing through our respective hangovers.

'Smell that air,' I say, 'it smells of freedom!'

'It smells as it always does, of tannery pollution.' N has one of those noses that actually bends when he wrinkles it. As we leave the Chaar Lumber Bridge, N turns to me and grins. 'You will miss the honeymoon period.'

I nod wryly. 'Yes, I'll be sitting in New York as Didi turns this place into London.'

The taxi makes its way through Rajarhat, Kolkata's burgeoning Gurgaon satellite township. N looks around at the isolated glass-and-concrete structures rising out of morning-fresh green flatland.

'You know, all this was Gautam Deb's,' he says, mentioning the CPM leader who's garnered the maximum amount of news coverage on his way to defeat. 'This was all Gautam Babu's to distribute as he saw fit.'

'All of Bengal was supposed to be his,' I reply. In the press, Deb was touted as the chief minister-in-waiting who would take over a year or so after Buddhadeb Bhattacharya stormed back into Writers' Building.

His shiny head catching the rising sun, N starts to sing a ditty in Bangla.

'All this was Gautam Deb's but now it belongs to Mamata! All this was Comrade Deb's but now it belongs to Didi!'

The taxi driver looks at us and grins.

'*Thik-i bolechhen, dada! Kissui paltabey na! Ei deshe'r kono poriborton hotey paarey na!*' You're completely right, dada. Nothing's going to change. There can be no transformation in this land.

I hope the man is wrong but I suspect he is right.

Epilogue: The Cobra of Power – An Opera

Notes for an operatic play, working title: The Thirty-Four Year Circus/The Cobra of Power, Bangla title: *Choutrish Bochhor'er Pala/ Khomotaar Keute.*

The stage would need to be huge, even Rabindra Sadan would be too small, so perhaps two or three interlinked pandal-stages on the Maidan, each at least five storeys high, with the audience sitting in the centre as the action moves from stage to stage. The cast would run into a hundred-odd actors. The 'opera' would mix styles from all the different genres of theatre we've known in Bengal over the last half-century: Tagorean verse-theatre, Sombhu Mitra's proscenium realism, Utpal Dutta's melodrama, Badal Sircar's Third or Free Theatre, Grotowski via Khardah, the best elements of Arun Mukherjee's cinematic *Jagannath* and so on, not excluding the traditional forms of Jatra, Bohurupi,

Khemta Naach, Chhau and Putul Khela, nor the popular forms of the circus, PC Sorcar magic shows and the Bolly-Tolly dance shows.

One narrative thread would be the Bengal of recent months, say from the massacre at Netai through the World Cup win to the election campaign. In and out of these scenes would run two contrapuntal themes of history: the CPI(M) and the Left Front from 1977 onwards and the Mamata-Trinamool from the late 1980s onwards with a small prequel from the '70s. Occasionally the rest of the world would make an appearance in stills and film on background screens: events such as major assassinations, the fall of the Berlin Wall and the collapse of the Soviet Union, the shifts in China, the rise of religious fundamentalisms, Babri Masjid, 9/11, India Shining, and so on, everything, in short, that would be needed to provide the bass-line of the *'Bairey'* to the *teevra 'Gharey'* of West Bengal.

Possible first scene, 1977 (the end of Emergency): On a dark, empty stage, a few men wearing rags fall out of jail gates and into the spotlight. We see that the dirty white rags are imprinted with the repeated motif of the red hammer, sickle and star. As the men blink in the light, above and behind them an Ambassador-*palki* carries an old man who is waving at crowds. A young woman leaps on the bonnet of the Ambassador and begins to dance in protest but the noise of her stamping gets lost in chants of 'Jaiprakash! Jaiprakash!'. Every now and then, throughout the play, this girl dancing on the Amby bonnet will pass through, the noise of her *taandav* getting louder and louder till, at the end, the palki (always empty after its first entry), is itself on a long 'Rajdhani train' and the noise becomes deafening. In the meantime, the men in rags develop crisp dhuti-panjabis. But their white clothes are always patterned by the red hammer and sickle. Across the play, the dhuti-panjabi men grow in number. They develop absurdly long Brahmin *chotis* and outsize red-brown Stalin moustaches. They all wear thick, black-framed spectacles. They dance in a lock-step *kirtan* and always speak or sing in a chorus. So, for instance, when the Berlin Wall falls, their Stalin moustaches, too, fall off, but they pick up the moustaches and put them back on, strictly in unison.

In the storyline of 2011, the first scene would be a small group, in various white costumes but patterned with the hammer and sickle, cowering in a house as a surging mass of people surrounds them. The small group opens fire, shooting through the windows in panic and people in the crowd outside fall to the ground.

Next in the longer story would perhaps come Morichjhanpi in the winter of 1978–79, the shifting island of silt represented by a massive, unstable brown bean-bag from which people tumble off as they are shot by police, the men in the hammer-sickle dhuti-kurtas dancing past, mouthing Marxist phrases. On a parallel stage, scenes of the positive things done by the Left, packets of soil passing from hand to hand as Operation Barga is launched, the first steps in *panchayati raj*, the army trucks rolling around Bhowanipur to protect Sikhs after Indira's assassination, people not having to sleep on empty stomachs in village huts for the first time. But then would come the tableau of one of the dhuti-panjabis sitting, drinking his Scotch as, behind him, a huge, three-storey-high blackboard with the English alphabet is erased by masked players swinging on trapezes. On another stage would be the huge crumbling walls of the old metropolis with ugly new blocks sprouting between cracks and beginning rapidly to crumble themselves. The grander action would be interspersed with intimate, realistic scenes from village, mofussil and crowded city, the family relationships changing, the anger and violence growing, the young leaving, the *pada* boys interfering and controlling daily lives, all this unfolding as the factories in the background come to a grinding halt, one by one. The chorus rises: *'Bengal is lazy! Bengalis are lazy!'* At one point a huge tractor would be hauled on to one stage while a huge computer appears on the adjacent one. Showing huge energy, the dhuti-panjabis with help from others dismantle both tractor and computer, the first being reduced to a large, rusted sickle and the latter to a huge, battered hammer. The chorus continues: *'Bengal is lazy! Bengalis are lazy!'*

On one stage, appears a large, papier-mache Cong-I hand standing vertically. There is the sound of tearing as an older Mamata Banerjee rips open the palm and steps out, sloughing off tri-coloured confetti and presenting an unsmiling nomoshkar to the audience. Another actress playing Mamata is carried across the stage lying goddess-like on a large BJP lotus. Another group of actresses, say five of them playing the current MB, lead simultaneous padayatras that criss-cross each other over all the stages, burying the small vans carrying the CPM leaders. As the girl goes by jumping on the bonnet of the Ambassador, one or two of the Mamatas ignore her, while the other three turn and stare at her with annoyance. As the lotus passes by again, two of the Mamatas combine to tear it to pieces. As the ripped Cong-I hand passes, two MBs take large swathes of tape and stitch it back together again. The soundtrack is taken over by the slap of hawaii *chappals* moving rapidly on asphalt. As the crowd churns around the five Mamatas, the massed bodies turn into a huge, human 'helicopter' that flings a Mamata out here and another one out there. We don't hear any words as the Didis begin to speak, we just hear a shrill, angry whine of many voices that rises in volume as the different episodes of Left Rule are played out.

Women are stripped and made to walk naked through the lanes of places marked Bantola and Birati in vibrating neon. Other red neon signs mark out Nandigram and Singur. Peasants are killed by cadres, women are raped, police open fire on people armed with sticks. The Stalin moustaches dance their unified kirtan, stringing along barbed wire made from *shola* pith that transforms into razor wire as the opera progresses. At one pivotal point in the current election story, one of the Stalin moustaches comes to the mike and makes comments about Sonagachhi and *bhatar*s, lewdly thrusting his pelvis backwards and forwards. To which a group of actresses dressed as sex workers also thrust their pelvises while chorusing, 'We don't know about bhatars, but Comrade Babu, you just lost a few lakh vhotaars!'

Towards the end of the play, a large see-saw becomes another device. On one end is a dhuti-panjabied, choti-bearing, black-*choshma*-wearing, red-brown Stalin moustached Comrade Babu and on the other is one of the actresses playing Mamata. At first, the Moustache Comrade is far heavier. Balancing on top of him are 'goondas' in T-shirts and pants and 'businessmen' in suits and safari suits, but all decked out in the hammer-sickle pattern, and Mamata goes flying. The heavier the red side gets the higher flies the lone Mamata figure, but she always lands back on the see-saw. As the play nears the end, the balance changes – one by one, the goondas and businessmen leap over and balance on MB's shoulders, gradually evening out the weight, revealing that their other side is patterned in green-and-orange cloverleaf.

On one stage, large digital signboards appear among outsize banana trees, flicking words: *Phase 1, Phase 2, Phase 3, Voter Turnout*, and then corresponding numbers. The paramilitary troop up and down the stages as the campaign speeches rise in crescendo. OB vans wind through the audience. Voters rush from one leader to another, form queues, come out looking at their marked fingers. Through this frenzy, the chorus continues: *'Bengal is lazy! Bengalis are lazy!'* The Mamatas gather together and sit, one playing with her I-pad, one with her mobile phone, one cooks, one paints, all are calm. The kirtan line of Dhuti-Panjabi Babus dances in attempted triumph but they are not convincing, all are holding on to their moustaches. As the results come in, one of them breaks from the line and says: 'Was barely able to catch a grass snake, tried to grab a cobra! Hah!' A man, wearing a tattered hammer-and-sickle-patterned kurta stumbles on to stage wearing a heavy-looking Writers' Building on his back. A kindly passer-by says, 'Here, let me cut off this tumour that is debilitating you. You will feel much better.' He lops off the building from the tattered man's back. The girl who's been jumping on the Ambassador bonnet carries a snake basket to the gathering of the five Mamatas. 'Here, Didi! This is yours now!' She says, as a large cobra sways up from the basket. 'What's this?' They ask the girl. '*Eita Khomotaar Keute*! *Shaamle raakhbey*!' she replies. This is the Cobra of Power. Keep it carefully.

List of Photographs

Glossary

Alimuddin Street: CPI(M) state headquarters

Andolon, Andolan: movement, campaign

Baam Phront, Baam Phont, Bum-Phrunt: the Left Front alliance of parties led by the CPI(M)

Bandh: strike, shut-down of city or region

Bangla ranna: Bengali cooking

Basti: working-class settlement

Bhadralok: supposedly genteel, educated Bengali/Calcutta 'middle-class'

Bhaja'r Dokaan: shop selling fried snacks

Bhatars: tricks, customers of prostitutes

Biradari: brotherhood

Boktita: speech, political address

Bondhugon: friends

Boti: traditional Bengali fish-cutting cleaver on wooden platform

Chakravyuha: a circular, labyrinthine battle-trap from the Mahabharat

Chappal/s: slippers

Choshma: spectacles

Choti: tuft of hair at the back of clean-shaven heads of Brahmins

Chowrasta: crossroad

CISF: Central Industrial Security Force

CO: Commanding Officer

CRPF: Central Reserve Police Force

Daab: green coconut

Danda: batons, bamboo sticks used by the police and security forces

Darwan: guard, gate-keeper

Dhaba: traditional north Indian roadside eatery

Dhokafies: clubs (v.)

Dhuti Panjabi: *dhoti*, traditional Indian wrap-around nether garment for men; *Panjabi – kurta*, long shirt worn over dhoti or pyjamas

DIG: Deputy Inspector General

EC: Election Commission

EU: European Union

Gali: lane

Genji: sleeveless vest

Ghughu paakhi: Spotted Dove

Ghugni: boiled chick-pea snack eaten all over Bengal

Haandi: cooking pot

Harmad: gangster

ITC: Indian Tobacco Company

Jhaamela: messy or knotty situation, incident, argument, fight, riot

Jhund: mob, cluster or people

Kaalboishaakhi: seasonal thunderstorms typical to the Bengal area, also known as 'Nor'westers' for the direction from which they come

Kaata-rasta: 'cut road', as in road blocked by felled trees, rocks or ditches

Karkhana: factory

Khawr: thatch

Kirtan: group singing of devotional songs

KKR: Kolkata Knight Riders, the Calcutta team for the IPL 20-20 Cricket League

Kokil: Koel

Ma, Maati, Maanush: 'Mother, Soil, Humanity' – the Trinamool's main election slogan

Ma-bonera: mothers and sisters

Maath: field

Mama/mamas: nominally uncle, mother's brother, Bengali slang for cops, beat policemen

Moddho-bitto: middle-class

Muri: puffed rice, either eaten dry by itself or with onions, boiled potatoes, oil, tamarind and chillies etc. Common street snack all over Bengal.

NTPC: National Thermal Power Corporation

OB: Outdoor Broadcasting

OC: Officer-in-Charge

Oposhonshkriti: obscene culture

Oppodartho: useless, unproductive, barren

Paalki: palanquin

Paara, para, pada: neighbourhood, locality

Pandal: pavilion made from bamboo and cloth

Pat, Patachitra: traditional Bengali scroll-paintings, usually accompanied by narrative songs

Patuas: painters of *pats*

Potaka: flag

Poriborton, Parivartan: change, transformation

Pradakshina: circumambulation

PWD: Public Works Department

RPF: Railway Protection Force

Samarthan: support

SDO: Sub-Divisional Officer

Shaadhu-bhasha: language of the sadhus, i.e. cultured speech

Shegun: teak

Shindur: vermilion powder traditionally worn by married women in the parting of their hair

Shobbhota: civility

Shroddha: faith

Sombhu Mitra: great director and actor of the Bengali stage

SPG: Special Protection Group, which escorts high-level politicians in India

SSU: State Security Unit, a local version of the SPG

Sushil shomaaj: civil society

Taandav: dance of destruction

Teevra: sharp (as in musical scale)

Acknowledgements

This election diary came about at the suggestion of and commission by the editorial team at *The Telegraph,* Calcutta. At the paper, I would like to thank Aveek Sarkar, Rudrangshu Mukherjee and, most of all, Sumit Das Gupta who bore the brunt of dealing with this erratic freelancer during one of the busiest periods of news-gathering in the last three decades.

This series could not have been written without unstinting support from R. Rajagopal and his desk team, the reporters and bureau chiefs at *The Telegraph*: Arnab Ganguly, Alamgir Hossain, Avijit Sinha, Vivek Chhetri, Kunal Sengupta, Devadeep Purohit, Manini Chatterjee and Sujan Dutta. Most special thanks also to Sanjoy Chattopadhyaya who went way beyond the call of duty as a photographer and journalist to accompany and advise me on my journeys both inside and out of Calcutta.

The steep increase in my knowledge and understanding of politics and recent history in Bengal comes from the extreme generosity of V. Ramaswamy, Ranabir Samaddar, Dwaipayan Bhattacharyya and, last but not least, Nilanjan Bhattacharya. I would also like to thank Ranu Ghosh and Indra Das for their support across this time.

To Amita Baviskar, the most distilled gratitude for being there, for her patience, for helping me de-clutter my thoughts and prose, and for giving me the confidence to look and write.

Finally, a massive thanks to Karthika V.K., my editor at HarperCollins, for having the idea of turning this into a book and then for having the good-humoured tenacity to make sure I managed to stitch it together.